LEADER WITHIN

CRAIG MARTELLE

Editing services provided by Lynne Stiegler
Cover by Ryan Schwarz
Formatting (both eBook and paperback) by Drew Avera
Beta Readers/Insider Team
Micky Cocker
Kelly O'Donnell
John Ashmore
Dr. James Caplan
James Slater

This book is a work of non-fiction.

Published by Craig Martelle, Inc
PO Box 10235, Fairbanks, AK 99710
USA

❀ Created with Vellum

INTRODUCTION

Who am I to write a book on leadership?

Nobody. Somebody.

Just like you.

Leadership is inside you, not outside. It's not a mask you wear.

Being a lighthouse on a stormy night doesn't take heroics. It only takes surviving the storm to show the light for those who are lost.

Leadership is hard like that. Simple in words. Not so easy in execution.

It never is.

Why are there people you wouldn't follow, not even out of curiosity? You know who they are.

Don't let that leader be you. The more you command, the less you lead.

Be the beacon and show the way.

I've been in leadership positions throughout my life, but too often, I didn't fill the role. Not until I fully embraced the understanding that it wasn't about me. That was when I started to make a difference.

When your time comes, will you rise to the challenge? If you're already in a leadership position, can you do better for your people?

This book is filled with snippets and anecdotes that will hopefully help you on your journey to be a better leader. We can all improve.

Take the first step and keep going.

It's like building a pyramid, but you'll never reach the top because the power is in building and growing, not in placing that last brick. The top is a place to stand where you can reach higher.

I'm not going to belabor any points in this book. Why would I? To impress you with my wisdom?

This is the philosophy I've learned the hard way—by making lots of mistakes. This is a journey from bad to good to making a difference in people's lives.

The epitome of leadership is when the people you're responsible for make it to their goals. You don't need to be up there. You only need to help them see the way and encourage them to go.

They will, and they'll be better for it.

So will you.

This book will be a little motivation and a little inspiration. There are things to think about on your journey and actual things I did on mine to deliver the results my team had to get.

WHAT IS YOUR PURPOSE?

Desired leadership mindset: **Know why you're doing it**

The decision to be a leader isn't yours to make. Sometimes, you get promoted into a position where you have to lead. Other times, it's because a job has to be done. Sometimes you want it, other times you don't. It's like a marriage, for better or worse.

Leadership fills a void.

You do what must be done, and then you decide to do it better. People start looking to you.

You. You're where the buck stops.

That's where leadership is found. Not all leadership starts with "good." Bad leaders get called a lot of names other than "bad leader."

No one gets up in the morning and says, "Today, I think I'll be a leader."

Maybe narcissists think that, but they wouldn't pick up a book like this since they already have the answers. If you know you're a narcissist, please return this book for a full refund. There's nothing here for you.

Everyone else, keep reading.

A phrase I often use is a quote from John F. Kennedy. "*A rising tide lifts all boats.*" For leaders, it is the ultimate truism. Everyone needs to rise together. Standing on someone else's back may help you over the wall of a prison, but you're leaving people behind, people who helped you reach a goal. That's not the way to do it.

If you want to go fast, go alone. If you want to go far, go together.

You have to bring the whole team with you to that better place, or it's not worth the trip. Remember, you win together. Even if there's strife, you can't be demeaning.

Tearing someone down never makes you better.

Leadership isn't a game of buzzword bingo, leveraging synergy to maximize core competencies. Leadership is about helping people become more than they are. It's about satisfying mutual needs. It's about successes both great and small.

That's the big secret to leadership: *It's not about you.* You will practice the best leadership when you look outside yourself. Helping others is a good cause regardless of what you get out of it. Helping others with a focus on how it can be mutually beneficial is getting closer because you both have a greater commitment to what you're doing.

They call it "buy-in." When everyone on the team has it, magic happens.

When you accomplish a shared goal but celebrate the *other* person's role when you reach those goals, you'll feel different about the end result.

How does it make you feel when you celebrate others' successes as much as your own? Enjoy their happiness. When you are sincere in your gratitude, people will want to work for you. People will want to help you. Make it about them by showing them what great looks like. Imagine yourself pointing at the goal and everyone looking at it. Together.

Don't think of yourself as being out front, pulling them after you.

That might have worked in the Marine Corps, but waving your arm for everyone to follow you has no power in the private sector unless your people believe in the goal.

Leading by example isn't standing out front either. It's about grabbing the rope and starting to pull. If the others believe it needs to be done, they'll join you. If they don't, it's time to reframe the need.

Help them share the goal. Stand together, side by side, and show them why it's important to *them.*

You might ask about the difference between a manager and a leader. A leader inspires. A manager handles the daily grind and is more a slave to process than a visionary. I used to be an outstanding manager.

Then I got a clue. It's not about me and the technical details of making a project happen. It's about getting people excited to participate, even if it seems mundane. Some work only requires managers, those people who oversee that everything is done the same way, day in, day out.

If you want to inject life into the process, encourage a few of your employees to set up a party for the team on the company dime on company time.

You'll see ingenuity and excitement—a celebration for something that matters prepared by those who believe. Become more than a manager who checks boxes while making sure everyone stays in theirs. Nothing more. That's what managers will give you.

You might find an inspirational leader who isn't in a

position of authority, but they are still leading. What are they doing differently? They aren't managing. They are showing people a better side of life. They are changing attitudes.

Because that's what leaders do.

You'll see in the following pages that I reference authors a fair bit, but that's because my current role is leading a group of nearly fifty thousand authors. This book is for everyone in a leadership role. Everyone has the opportunity to inspire and achieve things together that you would never be able to accomplish alone. The whole is greater than the sum of the parts.

Because that's what great leaders do.

2

VISION

Desired leadership mindset: **Help others see your vision**

Great leaders have great vision, even if that vision seems simple. If it unites a group toward a single purpose, it is great, no matter whether it is complex.

A group's vision goes to the core of its existence. With too many tendrils, the vision loses clarity. The group members lose focus. Here's a secret—you can only have a single number one priority. When goals conflict, different people will make different decisions. The organization gets pulled in more than one direction.

Take this, for example—the safe production of dynamite.

Dynamite can be produced safely. Can an employee stop the production line if they see an unsafe condition? The answer better be yes. If a leader waffles about it even for an instant, how do you think that employee is going to feel? They are going to have doubts. The leader has created a dichotomy.

Without consistent reinforcement of a single vision, one employee might push through, and another will risk stopping the line. Dissenting voices. Cracks in the armor. Don't let it happen to you. Be clear and consistent.

A good vision helps your people stay on track without second-guessing themselves.

Michael Anderle started 20Booksto50k® with two premises: don't be a dick and no self-promotion. After a year, I took over the leadership of the group. We had five thousand members at the time. As of today, we're closing in on fifty thousand. The rules remain the same, but we needed to refine how people saw the group to keep our conversations on topic.

This is the group motto now.

The business of being a self-published author.

It keeps us away from distractions and detractors. Success breeds an odd type of person. There are those who want to tear down something that is working. There are trolls who can't believe someone else can be successful, especially if the troll has tried and failed.

"You're just lucky."

I'm sure you've heard it before. I heard it just yesterday when a person made a litany of excuses for why their books weren't selling. "I'm an artist. I don't care about the money."

Michelangelo was an artist, too, maybe the best the world has ever known. And he was paid for his work. Artists get paid to produce art; otherwise, you're an amateur. Don't join a business group to attack the premise that artists deserve to make money from their work. That's a person trying to tear down what someone else has built. Their goal is not my goal.

Have a vision your people can buy into. Call it leader marketing because it is a leader's reality. You, as the leader, are charting the course. Your people are implementing it. If you're getting frustrated with the implementation or if you have to explain it, then it's not a good vision.

Think of Napoleon's Corporal. He would explain his battle plan to a corporal, who would recite it back. If the corporal understood it, Napoleon had confidence that it would be implemented as intended. He didn't have instantaneous communication, so he needed to establish the framework within which his people operated. With training before the battles, Napoleon's army was ready and successful on a military level. To conquer a thing, we have to know the thing.

Amateurs talk tactics, and professionals talk logistics.

You have to be able to implement your good ideas.

The business of being a self-published author.

That is how we framed the biggest self-publishing group in the world.

We stayed focused on a digestible purpose. It was how we grew tenfold and more. Being the talent. Being the chief of marketing. Being the back-end technical support and head of administration. All of it, but with the single goal of bringing your books to more and more people willing to pay money for them. That was a cause everyone could rally around.

From the Marines to the corner office to a self-publishing empire that works with other authors to help them realize the most value from their words.

The vision: *the business of being a self-published author*. If your self-publishing business isn't important or not a business, you're in the wrong place. Eliminate the distractions.

I demand a lot from myself. I feel like I have to show the way. If someone asks, I need to have first-hand knowledge. I'll show them what's possible. I'll show them the steps it takes.

How they take those steps is up to them.

I learned that lesson in the Marine Corps, too. Don't ask your people to do anything you wouldn't do yourself.

Vision is what sets leaders apart from managers, but how do great leaders find their vision? Maybe they see it in a dream or when they're thinking of something else, or through trial and error when other visions fail. Or someone shoots holes in them. A vision is the tracks down which your train rolls. It provides for the smooth operation of your team.

Safe production of dynamite. That's fairly weak, but it should suffice to guide all manner of what happens in the plant. *The business of being a self-published author.* It keeps the train rolling.

Steve Jobs' vision was *a computer for the rest of us.* It guided the company through ups and downs and to atmospheric in its growth when that computer became your phone. That computer became a small device that contained all the music you owned. Steve Jobs had other visions, too. Change the world. Technology that people can use. It all came together.

Vision is inspirational. What inspired you to do what you're doing? What will keep inspiring you? Take that and carry it over to the business or your team. Your business doesn't have a vision? Create one and embrace it. *A computer for the rest of us.* Beautifully simple yet profound.

Are you building a playground for your homeowners' association? *A place for our children to play.* IT need not be more complex than that. It should not be. You don't need to outdo the playground of the next neighborhood over. Comparisonitis is the thief of joy. Do right by you and your team.

When the pandemic started to rage, people began to flail. A calming voice is the lighthouse with the beacon. That was what we provided in our group. This was my message to them on March 21, 2020.

He who shows a case of ass during this crisis will suffer mightily. Even if you aren't calm, you must project it. Your readers, even if you only have ten, will rally around a voice of reason. The only thing you can control is your reaction to events. Make sure that when the dust settles, you aren't embarrassed at what you said. Hoarders? Who is to determine that? Is that person handicapped who is parked in the slot? None of that is your call. What if someone bought TP for their neighborhood of oldsters—ten packs going to ten different couples, yet the good Samaritan would suffer under the withering glares of judgment. We don't allow conversations about other's work in here—I may not like 50 Shades of Grey, but 125 million sales suggest I'm not the target audience. What I think doesn't matter. Eyes on your own paper. I listen to input regarding my writing from people whose opinions I value. And I adjust accordingly.

There are angry people out there, depressed folks, bargainers, those living in denial, and others who seem to take it all in stride. Those are the five stages of grief. Allow yourself to go through them. Reach out to your closest friends and talk through your pain. But recognize what it is. When online, be the rallying point for friends, family, and fans. Don't be that guy who is screaming into the wind on a video that goes viral. Nerves are frayed. Look outward, not inward. It is the armor by which every Marine shields himself. I can't be wasting time with no stages of grief! Jump right to the end and move on:) Here's a secret. I'm not immune. My dog passed away in January and took a part of my soul with her. My heart is permanently damaged, too, as I discovered from my heart surgery only three days later. No one can do anything about that. It is my issue to deal with while the world continues to turn, and turn it will, regardless of whether I'm there or not.

Choose to turn with it. Authors understand what it's like to work alone. Help your family and friends who are not. If you believe that you need to be there for them more than they need you, you will do just fine and you'll find out that you have as much support as you will ever want. Helping others is one of the greatest things you can do to help yourself.

Do you launch or not? Are your sales down? What do I do?!?!?!?! Keep a cool head and carry on, inside, from the sanctity of your own home. You have a business to run, so run it. Create new content and then sell the shit out of it. That's what you do. And there is a massive buffet of things to try, right here in 20Booksto50k(R). Some may work better than others but doing nothing for your business will get you nothing. Make the money now while people are inside because when the doors open again, people are leaving and may not read as much then as they are over the next couple months.

Be the rising tide. Be the lifeline that others can reach for. And manage your business. You're an indie. You've written a book, and that means you are a stalwart soul.

And that leads us to goals. Above, I set the vision for what I thought was a short-term effort, but as I write this book a year later, the trials and tribulations of 2020 continue. But we still have our businesses to run, and our businesses need us to run them.

Adjust and keep moving forward while staying true to your vision. That is what will keep you above the noise of distraction.

Whether you are a leader of one to a leader of many, establish your vision and stay the course.

3

THE GOAL

*Desired leadership mindset: **Clearly articulate** the **goal***

There's a book with that name (*The Goal* by Eliyahu M. Goldratt). It talks about a factory process and the theory of constraints written in a story-like narrative. The main point is to have the right goal.

You're in charge. Now what? You were put in charge for a reason. Whether it's the kids' annual school fundraiser or refurbishing your factory line, you have to know what the goal looks like, and you have to know it well enough to articulate it easily.

Begin with the end in mind. What does success look like? That is your starting point and your end point. It is easiest to articulate where you're going because you've already been there, at least in your mind's eye.

Everyone on your team needs to marry their goals to the vision and your project/team/mission goal. The individual goals are the building blocks for the group goal.

If your goal is to build a playground, individual team

member goals could be to secure the heavy construction equipment to prepare the ground, buy the playground equipment and have it delivered, rally the construction volunteers with the right tools, determine the layout, prepare lunch for the team, and more. If you have done any project management (I guarantee you that you have), this will be obvious. Individual goals are the building blocks of the project.

As your projects become more advanced, like increasing the number of widgets produced by your line at the factory, individual goals look more like a Kaizen process improvement event. How can you work faster without working harder? It's not about working faster, it's about producing more product of acceptable quality. To reach your goal, what if you could streamline the parts management process to make sure everything you need to do your job is within easy reach? The process it takes to reach your goal is one small gear in a much bigger machine. You can accomplish your job without working as hard at it because you've streamlined your range of motion.

This is where we all fit. Buy into the vision, build the goals. Deliver. And do it again.

Without individual steps between where you are and where you want to go, the project is wishful thinking. That is a goal without a plan. If hope is your plan, you have a lousy plan. You need to do better by the people who are counting on you.

You're in charge. You don't have time to be watching the grass grow. You need to detail the steps between here and there. Imagine trying to drive your car if you could only see a car-length ahead. That's exactly what it's like if you don't keep your goal in view. It's what micromanaging looks like. Pretty soon, you're off-course, and it'll be your fault.

The steps might deviate, but every step you take should get you one step closer. If you feel like you're spinning your wheels, you are. If you feel like you're taking baby steps, you are, but those are okay. Enough of those, and you'll get where you're going.

Work smarter, not harder, to get to the goal, but you might find that there are no shortcuts. If there is a better way, your people will help you find it. You don't need to take credit for it.

Reaching the goal together is why you're in charge. It has to be "we" working on "our" plan. That is how you reach your goal.

If you're marching forward smartly but your goal is getting fuzzy, it's probably best to stop until you can clearly see your goal once again. Sometimes you need to change your goal but think long and hard about why. If your answer is "it makes me look better," it's not a good goal. How much extra work does it take to hit a different goal?

Beginning with the end in mind is the perfect setup for realizing the best target for your group. Let me give some examples.

In the Marine Corps, we weren't given such pedestrian orders as "take that hill." That's not a mission-oriented goal that can adjust to a changing situation. We were given better orders like "deny enemy access," which afforded the small-unit leaders a chance to exercise their initiative to meet the bigger goal of winning the battle and winning the war.

I hope no one is shooting at you during your inexorable march toward your goal. That should make it a little easier.

When COVID-19 hit the world, I was running the

20Booksto50k® Facebook group. We had some 44k members, all authors either established or budding. When people had to stay home, it threw a large number of lives into turmoil. Some were able to leverage the time to improve their author business, while others now had children at home to homeschool, eating up time the author had been using to manage their business.

What kind of goal made sense to help the most people stay on track with their businesses? A mutual goal of getting to the other side without any pressure to produce. We held online sessions about revising goals. If people couldn't get their heads into a healthy writing space, we gave them a productive distraction. I started a daily hour-long talk show and interviewed fifty or sixty different people over the course of three months to bolster information resources. I gave away my non-fiction indie (self-published) author books for free. I gave away hundreds of audiobooks. I also donated money to authors in need. That started a groundswell with established authors sending me donations that I turned around. I started with a thousand dollars, and after two weeks, I gave out nearly $24,000 to authors around the world.

We did that again in December with a comparable result. When 2020 ended, I'd received $45,000 in donations and paid out over $50,000 in grants to more than two hundred and fifty people in need.

We did a lot of work to help people just make it to tomorrow.

Sometimes a loose goal makes the most sense. Other times, like when I worked as a business consultant, we needed to increase production by a target amount.

This was where we excelled. Study the processes for one to three months to identify the bottlenecks and opportunities. Leverage success. The production increase was something we talked about in executive meetings, but when the engine is hitting on all eight cylinders, the speed comes as a byproduct and not as a goal in and of itself. It's like magic when the individuals' goals align with the team's goals.

Those smaller goals made all the difference. We shared the overall production numbers with the front-line personnel to show them that what they did mattered, and we listened to them because they knew how to improve the processes.

Here's a business axiom to keep in mind when you're looking for answers to problems. *The ones closest to the action are in the best position to see what's going wrong and what is going right.*

Sounds like the Marine Corps. Put that checkbook away; there's more.

If you've ever heard of SMART goals, they start with these. They are the bite-size parts of the goal pie.

Specific (Exactly what is the deliverable)

Measurable (With a number that can be measured)

Achievable (It has to be doable)

Relevant (It has to apply to a bigger goal, and ultimately, the vision)

Timely (When you need to reach the goal)

Goals help you focus your energy. From a leadership standpoint, your people develop their own goals, which feed into the greater goal. Everyone wins.

But what if there's too much turbulence in the system?

Slow down. Ask your people why, and start looking at how to remove the obstacles.

A framework within which someone operates is not constraining. It's a necessity that levels the playing field for the spectacular to stand out. Look for great ideas that don't require a restructuring to implement. Risk versus reward demands a more calculated approach.

Which means scrutiny.

Pick the low-hanging fruit first. You'll find plenty of that. Those are the low-cost, high-impact process-improvement opportunities.

Scrutinize the framework within which the team operates and the vision that guides them. A process can always be improved. Always. Look at the pit crews in professional racing. Tenths of seconds make a difference. They train and equip themselves to get tasks done faster with greater consistency.

There's no reason your team can't explore efficiencies in processes. Ask them. They will know better than you. That's what the Kaizen process is all about—LEAN your process to eliminate waste. They are formal approaches to realizing greater levels of efficiency.

People have made careers and fortunes out of improving efficiency, and businesses have improved their bottom line. Investors and employees alike benefit when a company increases its profitability. Big ideas lead to the small processes that make them viable.

Clean out the pipes and let the engine run.

What does that have to do with goals? We started by talking about the right goal that you and your people are trying to reach. Can a single line worker improve a plant's production by ten percent? Probably not, and such a goal could be overwhelming. But everyone on the line working on little things in their control? That could deliver a monumental change.

You're the plant manager. How does your goal equal their goal? Give them a mission-type order. Turn them into more than workers just punching the clock. Help them become employees who are engaged in delivering at a higher level. That's good consultant-speak.

Set the right goals. From small to large, from personal to group, all of them driving toward a single point in the distance.

A point that you can see getting closer. Hitting each milestone toward your goal is worthy of celebration.

Every project requires a project plan, but not every plan needs to be extensive.

4

_____

THE LIGHTHOUSE

Desired leadership mindset: **Stand firm against the storm to show the way**

As the leader, you are the beacon around which your people must rally. In the darkness of confusion and change, you are the light.

During the pandemic months of 2020, my greatest efforts focused on providing a sanctuary for those whose lives were turned upside down. Somebody has to be positive and not by giving false hope, but by showing what is possible.

Like a flashlight in the darkness shows you what's there.

Exactly like that.

Act, don't react. The lighthouse doesn't wait for the storm. It shines whenever the sun isn't out. Act with purpose. Act with intentionality.

By keeping your vision foremost in your mind.

Reacting creates the conditions where you lose focus.

Bring the attention back through your vision to the goal and help the team stay on track, even if it means ignoring the storm. The storm is there regardless. Falling prey to it accomplishes nothing.

Don't be its victim. Take charge of your destiny.

The end of negativity comes when we stop criticizing others, comparing ourselves to others, and judging. Life begins when we see the good inside, learning from others to do for ourselves, and knowing ourselves. Helping others see the colors of this world and embrace its beauty.

Being positive is a choice. Make the best decision for yourself, your sanity, and your business. Here's a message I sent to the group in October of 2020.

Author's Self Care and Addressing the Trauma of 2020

Under a gibbous moon in the darkness of a winter sky, the stars are as radiant as ever.

Everything changes while also staying the same. Our role is small, but small is big when the impact is magnified from one to another. When I feel down, I do something for someone else because no matter what, there's always someone out there who is worse off, no matter how bad things are.

With loss comes the challenge of dealing with it. We all have emotions. Events affect us differently based on the experiences of our lives. Know yourself and what that means. Recognize that others will not respond as you do. Be kind to them. They're different from you. We're all the same in that we're different. We're all the same in that we need purpose.

Maybe your purpose is to help just one other person. But you're an author. Authors have the ability to help so many more through their words—whether they are words to help someone escape, threads to help one stay alive in hospice just to read the next story because they have to know before they go, or education to help people understand and better improve their lives. Your influence far outsizes a single person staring at a blank page that begs to be the embodiment of what's in your mind.

No one knows what the future holds except that it will be different, just like 2020 was different from all other years. Like 2021 will be different. How can you get ahead, stay in front of the curve in order to provide for your family? Flex more quickly when the world changes.

...

Look forward not back especially if there's too much pain. My good girl has been gone for ten months. It's every bit as hard on me as losing a parent or a sibling, probably more so. It's still hard. This year I've been almost fanatical in helping others, being a beacon to help dissipate my pain. It works, and it doesn't. Everything is different without her, but the stars still shine in the night sky because the universe is far bigger than just me.

My role, our role is in being the beacon for others.

To some, this has been their best year ever when it comes to author revenue. I salute you and cheer you on to higher and higher levels. To others, they feel like they've lost their mojo. It's still there, only hidden in the shadows. Shine the light to show it the way back to where it belongs.

If you need to, take the next month off from Facebook and the news. You'll be far healthier for it. The world is ending and the US on the brink of civil war! But we're not. Believe what you see with your eyes and wave to your neighbors as you drive by, even if they're flying a Chelsea flag in the middle of Man U's home turf. We're all different, but we're all the same. Everyone needs a beacon to find their way, and everyone needs something to hold on to.

A new home, a new job, a divorce, and so many things! Embrace the one constant in your life. Everything changes. Take control of what you can control and make it your foundation. Remember pizza Friday? So many families had that. We did. One thing to hold on to. And then one more. And then your story. Soon, you'll find that what has changed isn't as debilitating.

Look forward because that is the direction you're going. Time gives us no other choice. Only our minds can hold us in the past, and only our minds can free us.

5

THE LIGHTNING ROD

Desired leadership mindset: **Sometimes you have to be the lightning rod and diffuse the bad energy**

As the leader, you carry the full burden of everything your people do or don't do. If you think too hard about it, that responsibility will overwhelm you.

In the Marine Corps, we had the strategic corporal. That one individual could cause an international incident through a misdeed or just the perception of a misdeed. Sometimes the smallest things can make a big difference. Defusing an incident quickly is important for any leader. In the Marines, there were international implications. The worst thing to do was blame the frontlines. They could be corrected behind the scenes if their actions were against policy or procedure, but publicly, the leader had to stand up and take full responsibility while promising the powers that be it wouldn't happen again. Then there would be the necessary restitution.

In one case, that meant hurrying the individual out of

the country so they wouldn't be put in prison for the rest of their life for something that wasn't a crime in the US but was where we were. For the leaders, it wasn't about them, it was about their people.

When I was in Russia, one of our inspectors was snagged in a honey pot. He was single at the time, but they caught him unaware, and that innocent massage turned into a ninety-minute video of hot passion.

The Russian government officials summoned our office to look at the egregious damage done by one of our own. We were concerned until we saw what it was. High fives and cheers weren't exactly what our counterparts expected. "No one cares." We had just seen that in President Bill Clinton's impeachment trial where we were in Russia, and we used their own words against them. "It's just sex."

The leaders defused the situation because it had been artificially created in an attempt to exploit it. In this case, it was a diplomatic maneuver that found no traction because the leaders focused on the real issues at hand and refused to be distracted.

Sometimes you need to be the lightning rod because your people need to vent. Give them a healthy forum for that, then move on. That's what empathy is all about.

The Sales Unknowns during COViD-19

This is the one consolidated post for wondering about dips in sales, questioning your launch strategies, or learning that your chosen lifestyle is called "quarantine."

Who knows whether I should launch or not? The answer to that is no one knows. In my non-fiction books I talk about building a readership and managing reader expectations. A solid group of fans will insulate you from other market pressures (including time-of-year drops). If you don't have a fanbase built up, then that's what you need to do. Regardless of whether there's a virus sweeping the world or not.

How do you know if your book is any good or not if you don't put it out there? The greatest validation is from strangers in your genre reading your book. They will tell you through their actions or inactions, as in, you'll get good reviews or no reviews. I estimate one in every 100 to 250 purchasers will leave a review. Your worst reviews will come from any free giveaways. Just accept that fact—trolls and wayward souls live in Freeland.

Should you delay your launch? No one knows. I surely am not, but I have a good base readership and that gives me a nice launch regardless. It's what happens after that that matters. On Monday, my pre-order of the first in a new series goes live. I'll check to make sure that it is in KU and then I'm dropping the price to 99 cents for one to two weeks to put it in as many hands as possible. I've booked a great number of paid promotions starting Wednesday. I've worked a number of swaps with my peers. It is the most I've ever spent on a launch and it is far and away the greatest effort I've made with a new book. I started all of that two months ago. Book 2 is on pre-order. Book 3 will be when Book 2 gets uploaded. It's my master, hard-launch plan in execution. I still expect sales—lots of sales because it has a way sexy cover and decent blurb. I'm not delaying anything because I have a good plan.

Page reads will go up. I've been promoting the hell out of the two months of Free KU that Amazon is offering for newcomers (it is US only, but that is the biggest market—even if you're not in the US, bring those US subscribers on board). Page value may drop, but reads go up, then you may gain fans who will read your backlist or be jonesing for your next book when page values go back up. You must always be driving to gain new fans. Sometimes that comes at a cost, but you will always have a long-term financial windfall with an expanded fanbase. If you are wide, see what B.&N, Apple, and Kobo are doing.

Audible is letting child listeners enjoy children's books for free. How about that?

And this is the sole thread for lamentations regarding sales or anxiety or other things out of your control. Maybe you can focus on what is in your control? Comment on that, too. We'll remove all new threads regarding low sales during this time or launch heebie-jeebies because of quarantine or any of that which cannot be answered. Those create drama and friction. We don't need any of that and neither do you.

What about other controversial topics? Sometimes you need to take the heat generated by the project. There will be those who don't agree the project is worthwhile. When I worked in the oil industry, there were always protesters. The work crews performed admirably in the worst conditions. The company leadership stayed between the protestors and the work crews, being the lightning rod for negative press.

The front lines appreciated it. They were shielded by those who didn't have it in their job description to have objects thrown at them. The leaders did it because they were in charge, and it was a small price to pay to keep the project moving forward.

When criticism and heat come from on high, there is only one correct answer. "It's my fault." You are the leader. You are responsible for everything your people do and what they don't do. You have to believe in them. If something goes awry, take the blame before you dig into it. Nearly everything can be fixed.

I think my greatest leadership triumphs came when I was the Intelligence Officer for Marine Aircraft Group 11. I had three guys on my team who had been reduced in rank under non-judicial punishment. I also had one guy who had been court-martialed for theft of government property. I collected these broken people. I even used my coveted "Bydir" authority to transfer the one who had been court-martialed onto my team. "Bydir" means by direction of the commanding officer. His authority was that of a colonel, and I was only a first lieutenant at the time.

I used it on official letterhead. I didn't want to bother him with it, but I also didn't want to be told no since the sergeant's career was at stake.

I got my ass chewed something fierce for that and lost my Bydir authority, but the colonel didn't hold it against me and did not reverse the order. He was later promoted to general, and we maintained cordial relations for the rest of my career.

My team was an all-star collection of intelligence professionals. We looked like something out of *Kelly's Heroes*, but in the field, we always had communication, hot coffee, and the gouge (a Marine aviation term for the inside scoop because we conducted as much internal intelligence-gathering as external). We had staff meetings in my tent before the staff meetings because everyone came by for coffee and the latest gouge.

When I was with a different unit deployed in the Middle East, the commanding officer suggested the Marines could use a drink. He challenged me to put together a party complete with booze. There was no doubt that I was going to make that happen. We contacted the Marine House at the US Embassy, where alcohol was imported and kept on sovereign American territory. We checked out a bus from the motor pool and enjoyed a ninety-minute liberty at the Marine House, where everyone was able to enjoy a libation of their choice.

Or three. I was surprised at the damage some guys could do in that short a time span. But we persevered, and I earned a Naval Commendation Medal from that deployment.

I was the lightning rod because my team needed someone to believe in them. They were convinced early of how far I would go for them.

Being the lightning rod from internal distractions is something every leader will experience. People get emotionally charged. Expect it.

Divert, distract, and delay to dilute the emotional engagement that could blind people to the fuller picture, the big picture. Give them something else to see until their emotional high is tempered by time. Don't give people a chance to regret emotionally charged diatribes. Leaders have to save their people from themselves. Give them a different focus for a short while.

During the emotionally charged events of the summer of 2020, we simply shut the 20Booksto50k® group down while the angry voices drifted away, having lost the target of their ire. When we reopened the group, we had post control turned on so no one could restart the drama. The hostile voices disappeared overnight. We no longer had to fight fires as the trolls tried to destroy us. Tried to destroy a group that helps people of all shapes and sizes make a decent living by writing books.

Without caveats or discrimination of any sort. Sometimes there are more than two sides to an issue. I'm not with you, and I'm not against you. I'm doing this thing to help people earn a decent living.

The two sides that were offered? Neither gave me an option I could live with. I chose the third option, stayed above the fray, and let the emotions subside while we never stopped working. When those who were twisted with rage came back to themselves, we welcomed them. We never changed our goal of helping people provide for themselves and their families.

We maintained our vision. In this instance, there was

no value in being a lightning rod for a fight that was not ours. We came out much stronger than a great number of others who lost their way. Vision is critical, even if you take a few lightning strikes. Know where you're going, and you'll be able to keep moving forward.

6

EXPECTATIONS

Desired leadership mindset: **Temper expectations**

The vast majority of our grief comes from the difference between reality and expectations. Temper your expectations and help your people temper theirs. Of course, you plan to reach your goals, but the expectation of becoming a rock star while doing it has to be tempered.

Take a critical look at your life and see where you were the angriest or saddest and what made that so? Maybe you expected a promotion at work, and it went to someone else. Maybe you expected the person you liked to like you more.

It's difficult to temper expectations because hoping for the best is a human default. I once heard someone say, "I always expect the worst, and I'm never disappointed." I thought that was defeatist until I parsed it, then I decided it was genius. If you expect the worst outcome, you can work to mitigate that. With expectations set for the worst, anything better than that is a positive. It might seem like a contrarian view, but if you expect the best outcome, anything less will be a disappointment.

Don't be disappointed. Adjust and keep moving forward.

The happiest people go with the flow—not because they don't care, but because they manage their expectations. It starts with getting up in the morning and welcoming a new day. You can be happy or not. It's your choice.

As I get older, just waking up brings a certain amount of pain, but it lets me know I'm still on the right side of the dirt. I do my best to get the result I want, but when I don't, I use it as a learning point. What do I need to do to keep moving forward?

As a leader, helping your people temper their expectations starts with setting a goal they can reach. I'm sure we've all heard the expression, *"Aim for the stars because if you miss, you'll land on the moon"* or something like that. It starts with jumping off the ground, then getting into the sky, then to the upper atmosphere… You get the point. As a leader, you set the vision but then temper the expectations to meet each new goal as you rise until eventually the stars are within reach.

From inch stones to milestones, understand where you are, and keep your people from jumping ahead. Humanity likes shortcuts. Streamlining and process improvements are not shortcuts. They're good business. That is how you train your team. Motivational speeches need to have the foundation of a solid and implementable plan.

Skip too many steps, and all of a sudden, your plan becomes wishful thinking. Nothing more than hope, and hope is a lousy plan.

Your role is to keep people on track with their goals and their role in the group goals, based on a viable plan. That is what you need to communicate, day in, day out.

I wrote this to the 20Booksto50k® group. We all have our issues. It's not just you. But there are ways to get out of a rut and keep moving forward.

Being kind to yourself isn't the same as not pushing yourself when you know you need to push. But only you know that. Kick yourself in the pants if you need it, but don't if you don't.

I hit max fry and managed 6900 words written in seven days despite sitting at the keyboard for countless hours. My beta readers told me to shut my computer down. I finally listened and binged Deep Space Nine, and then a different new TV series, and a couple movies. I got back on track with 6900 words written in two days.

But that's me. For some with full-time jobs and families, 6900 words could be a good month's work. Celebrate your good work as you only compete against yourself. If a 7k month is a good month, then have one of those every month and be satisfied with your progress.

Most of our stress relates to expectations. If you expect 10k words and get 5k, you're upset. But if you expect 3k and get 5k, you're happy. Manage your expectations and the steps you take to meet them. Setting a goal is one thing, but the expectation is key. Don't set goals you can't reach. Getting 10k words in a day is a rare event for most people. I write every day and get 10k words far less than 1% of my writing days. There's a 99% chance to get less than 10k words. I never set a goal of 10k or even have expectations of 5k, but on a good day with a well-thought-out scene, I can hit 5k before lunch.

This goes to everything in your business. Make the steps to your goal the expectation and make them achievable. Work within your capabilities to get there. And most importantly, leverage what you're good at. Don't take that which is your arch-enemy and make it all you do for a week. That is setting yourself up for failure—punishing and torturing yourself. If you don't like something, take it in smaller, more palatable bites. Except peas. Even single bites of peas are disgusting. So change peas to snap beans and all is well.

7

THE RISING TIDE

Desired leadership mindset: ***A rising tide lifts all boats***

In the publishing industry, there is no zero-sum game. No one has to lose for you to win. When one author converts a TV-watcher to a reader, all authors win because a person can read far more books than an individual author can write.

Winning is a team sport where the only opponent is you and your drive to do a little better today than yesterday.

As the leader of a rising tide, you cannot carry people since you'd sink. You need to all rise together. That means everyone carrying their own weight, improving their own performance.

In the self-publishing world where we work as individuals, where we are responsible for all the elements of our businesses, how can that work?

We're all in the same boat and recognize that we have a lot more in common than what separates us. Banding together to share what has worked for us, share access to our readers, and share our successes makes us all stronger. "But…but…the competition!" some may shout.

I'll say it again. People can read a lot more than we individually can write. There's never been access to books like we see today. In the past, budgets were limited, and people had to plan to buy the next hardback by their favorite author that came out.

That business model is losing traction. More people are reading ebooks, and with Amazon's subscription-based model, they can read as many as they want for ten dollars a month (price as of February 2021). More and more people are reading. It is the cheapest entertainment out there.

For my fellow authors in military science fiction or space opera and me, we share each other's new releases and the latest news about our books. It's us against the television watchers, not us against each other.

Some might say that those who became the richest during the various Gold Rushes were those people who provided picks and shovels to the miners. That's partially true because a good supply chain will benefit any business. As the mines dried up and the miners moved on, the supply companies remained, turned shovels into plows, and added seeds to their orders. They helped build a different generation of people whose labor provided for their families and the families of others.

I live in Fairbanks, Alaska, where the riverboats brought the miners and their goods before those good people trudged inland. Their footprints are stamped all over this city, which was built to support them. Gold mines and dredges are still here, as is the city, but the only miners who remained were those who picked up another trade. They flexed and rose with the tide brought on by the Gold Rush.

How does any of that apply to leadership? Helping others help themselves. Showing what's possible. Leading when it's a group of peers.

And leading when it's about everyone in the group and not just you.

8

ESCHEWING ONESELF

Desired leadership mindset: **You are secondary to the group's goal**

"Trust is the new currency in leadership." Dr. John Blakey

Look at this as the sincerity of goals (no subterfuge). Some call it servant leadership. I prefer to think the leader is there to do a job that needs to be done. It might be more intellectual than what others on the team are tasked with. It might be more physical. In all cases, it is secondary to those who are moving the team forward.

You can't carry them on your back, as much as you might think that's the right answer. It isn't.

They have to buy into the vision, which requires that the vision not be about the leader.

When it's about the leader and not the team, it might be narcissism. Or megalomania. I'm not here to make a clinical diagnosis for anyone, but no one needs to give it a name. You've all seen it—the leader who makes it all about him.

Don't be that guy! Be the leader who convinces the team that the vision is worthy and the goals are attainable. The servant-leader will go farther than anyone who is in charge for purely selfish reasons.

No one is more committed than the leader. True, but that's not a reason to rub it in anyone's face. Be there working side-by-side with your team.

Even if you're in different cities and working independently. You as the leader should show up when you said and ask good questions and measure progress, keeping the vision in sight as the team keeps moving forward.

The only person on the team who doesn't matter as an individual is you, the leader. You become the face of the project, and you will feel the pressure of that burden. No one will be looking out for your needs.

But they will. Your team will take care of you when you are present for them, when you are consistent, when you listen to their input, and when they feel valued. Demand nothing. Accept what you've earned.

Even when you get nothing.

Eschew yourself, and you'll find your rewards are far greater than anything you could have demanded from your team. If you have a higher boss who is watching, make sure you give your team the praise they deserve.

Are intrinsic rewards worth it? Realizing success with a project is its own reward, and more so if you bring the entire team with you. You cross the finish line together.

When I worked as a business consultant, we spent years working with corporate leaders in heavy industry. They had high-paying jobs that were merciless, yet when they hit the production line to have sincere conversations with the people in the supply chain, the planning team, the production team, and the delivery team, they saw a marked improvement in team performance.

Being present has the greatest value and making it about someone other than the person in charge helped to deliver extremely high-dollar projects on time and on budget.

You can't demand respect. The only thing you can do is earn it, and once you have it, it's easily lost. Keeping the focus on the team will reduce your risk of running afoul of them. As long as everyone is moving forward together, when one stumbles, you hold each other up. It's a great concept and even greater to see it work.

The leader within is more than just you; it everyone on your team. The group motivates itself. The leader is the catalyst by shining the light on what's possible.

That's the beauty of eschewing yourself and living with good leadership principles.

In the Marine Corps, getting promoted meant moving farther and farther back in the chow line. When I became an officer, we saved time by starting at the back of the line. We usually ate the scraps of whatever was left over. And it was okay because when the rubber met the road, those who ate first did the heavy lifting. They needed to be ready. Contrary to popular opinion, officers did get their hands dirty, but not anywhere near as often as the lower ranks.

9

LEADING BY EXAMPLE

Desired leadership mindset: **Walk the walk**

The worst leaders embrace the principle of "Do as I say, not as I do."

The Marine Corps set that one straight in my first days. My drill instructors did everything they asked us to do, showing us how to do it, and they did it better and faster than we could imagine. It showed us what was possible.

Every Marine needed to do his job and the job of the next two levels up the chain of command. It was the Marine way because when the chips were down, one never knew who was going to be available.

So we learned it all up, down, and sideways.

And we were expected to be on our game at all times. The higher the rank, the more we had to play by the rules. That was why God created gunnery sergeants—so they could take care of anything that might be questionable without the officers getting involved. Or knowing, for that matter.

You don't need to be a Marine to lead by example. In our author group, I write and I publish. I sell enough books every single day to maintain credibility in the industry. That's what it takes.

What about a separate project where you are leading individuals across a variety of specialties? You listen to their input and do what's best for the whole team.

No one knows everything, and none of us are as smart as all of us when we work together. There's never a time where knowing it all is helpful. Experience teaches that wisdom is being aware of what you don't know.

Beware the person who portends to be an expert in all things, for those are the ones who order others to do as they themselves wouldn't. Because they can't; otherwise, they would be able to help with the understanding of a task's key elements. What to avoid. What to look for.

Sometimes the best thing a leader can do when managing a team of experts is to make sure the coffee is hot and the conditions are right. And then the person in charge has to facilitate the conversations. If that's you, you don't have to speak, only make sure that those doing the talking stay focused on the goal and true to the vision.

If you have to make a decision, make it based on the best information available and move forward. If you have to change a decision because you now have information that calls for a different course of action, make the call. The challenge with this is you can't be changing your mind with each new day. You get one change. After that, you'll look like you're guessing.

Don't let an artificial time constraint force you into making a too-hasty decision. That is one of the many elements that comes into play. Assessing the information and deciding what's best is what leaders do. It helps when everyone has bought into the plan. Or most, anyway.

What happens when the chips are down? I decided to write this book during the pandemic of 2020 because that was probably the greatest crisis most people would ever see in their lifetimes.

A crisis is a window into one's soul.

People had the opportunity to shine. Others would stay the course. And then there were the rest, many of whom became unhinged. If that was you, today is a new day. If that wasn't you, don't lord it over those who didn't do well during 2020, a year of crawling through broken glass for far too many.

What did I do? Led by example. I donated money to those who were grossly impacted by the pandemic. My intent was to help struggling authors. That turned into a groundswell of donations. It was important for me to give what I gave because I wasn't impacted by the pandemic except that I saved a lot of money by not traveling. 2020 was a net positive in my cash flow.

It wasn't a time to shepherd assets. It wasn't about "Hey, look at me, I'm donating money!" It was about doing right by my fellow humans. A lot of people joined me in that effort. We helped many through the hardest time of their lives.

When it was all said and done, we had done more than we said. And then we started a hearty cheer of "Get those books written! 2021 is a new year." Because we were helping people to help themselves, too.

How does this relate to a production facility or even a school board meeting? Show up early and make sure you did the work. For the meeting, make sure you read what you were supposed to and you're prepared. That you are ready for conversations that might be contentious. What do we want? Then the hardest question to answer is, "How do we get there?" It doesn't hurt to say what you don't want. I'll talk about that later, but suffice it to say, your example is in knowing what you need to know for that moment in time.

On the production line? It's about walking the safety walk and being able to have a conversation about what's important to those on the front line. Wear your hard hat. Wear your safety glasses. Show them why it's important.

Walk the walk.

Lead by example by being comfortable in your gear. It helps if it's a little bit dirty. Too many plant managers wear stuff that looks like it just came out of the gear locker. I still wear the coat I received as a gift in a plant. It is dirty and ripped, but it's my coat with my name embroidered on the front. It means the world to me. I could fit right back in at the plant.

It's a point of pride to get one's hands dirty with the people who are doing the work. I would sometimes help them clean up because it was a job that had to be done and one they didn't like very much.

When I was in Korea as the senior Marine Intelligence Officer, I kept my ear to the ground and read everything I could that came across the channels. Many were limited distribution, with only a handful of people able to read information based on restricted forms of collection to limit the chance of inadvertent disclosure. The sources could lose their lives if the information was compromised. With a buildup of intelligence from across the spectrum, I came to a conclusion that no one else shared. Something was going to happen that night.

I marched into the commanding officer's office and closed the door, interrupting other work he was doing. I briefed him on my conclusion. Although we had a limited role, he was armed with the information to discuss with the commander in chief at their next meeting.

That night, a North Korean mini-sub filled with Special Forces personnel got tangled in a commercial fishing net. The Navy raced out there and helped drag the submarine into port. The nine men inside died through murder-suicide before South Korean personnel could get inside.

On a one-year tour, that was the only time I briefed the colonel on an imminent threat. I earned credibility, which gave me a special place from which to lead intelligence personnel. Plus, that's what I was good at—reading mass quantities of disparate information to compile related points and draw a conclusion about future operations.

Everyone has their special skills, and that is what you leverage as the leader of any team. You don't need to know it all, you only need to know who to ask. Leverage your strengths and minimize your weaknesses. That is what leading from the front is all about.

There's also the part of you outside the workplace. Leading by example means retaining the respect you've earned in the workplace while not giving your team any reason to doubt you. Too many fall down in their private lives, and they wonder why their workforce remains skeptical of their motives. Everything you need to know about a person's integrity, you can see on the golf course. This is a fundamental element of a person's being. Cheat at golf. Cheat at life.

I don't keep score on the course because for me, it's about getting outside, hitting the ball, and making a good shot or two. It's not about the score. That's what people can learn about me on the golf course.Be the good person you need to be. If people can't manage their personal lives, how can they be expected to manage anyone else's? Know that on any project where you're in charge, you are taking over at least one aspect of other's lives.

Take the responsibility and lead by example in both private and public life.

Something to ponder on your leadership journey.

10

TAKING ACTION

*Desired leadership mindset: **Actions speak louder than words***

Although you might judge yourself on your intent, everyone else will judge you on your actions. So, make your actions count. Do what needs to be done, whether it is visible or not.

Working hard at something shouldn't look like you're flailing. That will get you judged more harshly than doing nothing. And that's why people spend so much time talking about a problem rather than defining and solving it. Why?

People are afraid to be wrong, and no matter what, you'll have critics.

Make no mistake. *You will be judged.* But it is important that you don't judge anyone else. It is human nature to judge people. Since you have to work in this world as it is, not as you wish it were, you have to keep your judgments to yourself while weathering the judging looks and unkind words of others.

Until your actions show what you are made of.

As Lou Holtz said, "When all is said and done, more will be said than done." Only you can change that paradigm. It takes doing and not talking.

In the Marine Corps, there's not a great deal of talking that takes place. Much of what Marines do requires physical engagement, even for Intelligence Marines. So much time spent wading through reports and staying in touch with the collectors in order to consume what they provide. Working angles and maintaining backdoor contacts because there were two separate lines of communication when it came to intelligence—the official chain, which was cumbersome and unresponsive, and the unofficial chain, which consisted of phone calls to buddies.

All of that was taking action. Of course, we filed the formal requests in order to cover our butts, but then we made the phone calls. When I was with the Marine Air Group 11 (MAG-11), I published the Air Intelligence Cookbook, and we sent hundreds of copies to intelligence shops worldwide. Everyone knew my name. When I called, they would talk to me.

When I served, I was in motion from dawn to dusk. I was the first in the office and one of the last to leave. I was always engaged with the current team. On the staff, I was generally a follower, but with my team, I was the leader. It was my responsibility to complete whatever tasks we were given, and we did. As a team, and I was there with them every step of the way.

Ask yourself how much time you spend thinking and how much time doing. You must think through the plan, and then it must become a plan of action. Many leaders sit around all day and talk, but they aren't you. You have a job to do.

In the 20Booksto50k® author group, I talk about this a

lot while also getting in my daily word count. I write every day and get a respectable number of words. I can't lead from the front if I'm not publishing. I can't be the lighthouse if I don't deal with the issues other authors encounter.

When it comes to leading by example and taking action, the rising tide starts with me. Actions. I want to earn your respect through my actions. I get to say the words, too, but I back them up. Fans of my fiction support me as well. It's important to me that I walk the walk.

Because actions speak louder than words.

11

ASKING QUESTIONS

Desired leadership mindset: **Ask to learn. Listen to move forward.**

A leader's most powerful tool is the willingness to ask questions.

But you have to listen to the answers. Loyalty is built with people who feel listened to. And why not? None of us are as smart as all of us. Once you've delivered your vision, your people will have ideas that will help you and your team realize success.

You don't have to build the engine. You have people for that. You only need to drive the boat, convincing the good people what their hard work will accomplish. But when you're driving the boat, you can't see what's happening aboard it. You can trust your instruments because they give a snapshot of what's going on. You can trust your people, too. Help give them the confidence to run what they are responsible for running. What if your power drops off? Do you give it a little more gas and think nothing of it? Maybe you could ask the chief engineer if there is something going on? I suspect you'll get a great deal of information. Listen and support your people.

I like this analogy because it works. Every system is made up of interdependent moving parts. When one changes, it affects all. In every group endeavor of my life, every contributing member of a team had to deliver on their part of the project.

Here was how I shaped the conversation surrounding good questions with my fellow authors.

You want to ask questions that elicit a conversation among professionals.

Questions that start with "So..." or "Have you heard..." are generally drama-inducing wastes of time. We seek a professional conversation about something that you personally know is real. Then you can bring that experience to bear to raise the value of the conversation.

If you can answer a question with 'yes' or 'no,' it's a bad question as it stifles the opportunity to learn. A binary question can be answered without conversation and can almost always be found with a minimum of research.

Open-ended questions are best, especially when backed with other facts surrounding the issue. An example is talking about what you did and how it turned out based on your expectations/projections. Ask, where did I go wrong?

...

The more specific the question, the better the conversation and the more likely the answer will solve your problem.

The broadest questions have almost no value and are a significant drain on our members. "I wrote a book, now what?" We decline all those questions. You need to help yourself before anyone else is willing to help you. We all have monumental workloads. No one has time to take on your workload, too.

Learn your business to help you ask better questions. You

don't have to love the business side, you only have to do it. And if your declined post makes you flounce out of here, then you need to take a good hard look at yourself to see if you're tough enough to work in this business.

Better questions do that. The level of professionalism in any group is dependent upon the quality of the conversations.

The questions are only the start; the willingness to listen is the catalyst for positive action. Listen to ask a new question, not to respond. Too many people are reloading before the speaker is done answering. You'll see journalists badger someone they are interviewing, never letting the person answer. This is annoying to watch and disingenuous. They want to fluster the interviewee. They want them to self-destruct and maybe admit to something sinister. But most of the time, the person simply gets irritated and storms off, which is good for ratings.

Such questioning techniques have no place in business or in a civilized world. Make sure you don't devolve to that level. Remember, you're the positive one, the person the team looks up to as a good example of helping the team help you.

Ask better questions, get better answers.

12

PROBLEM SOLVING

Desired leadership mindset: **Weigh risk versus reward**

Solving a problem is easy, isn't it? The leader makes the decision, and the problem is fixed. Not so fast. There are four questions to ask when it comes to solving a problem.

1. What is the problem?
2. What is the impact on time?
3. Assess the risk to safety (people and/or equipment)?
4. What is the cost?

The most important element in solving a problem is defining it.

A technique I like is beginning with the end in mind. I ask myself what a good resolution looks like. Can we pre-plan the solution to determine what it will take to resolve the problem?

When I worked with the Department of Homeland Security, one of our biggest problems was throughput at an airport checkpoint. Being in Pittsburgh, we had access to some incredible resources, and one such was a business management group out of Carnegie Mellon University (CMU). They studied the checkpoint and within a week, they put together a highly technical report that suggested the choke point was the passengers unloading their gear to go through the X-ray machine.

We added tables in front of the machines for passengers to prepare, and we added informational signs. What you see nationwide in the United States started at Pittsburgh International, thanks to clearly defining the problem. After that, resolving it took little budget and some ingenuity to rearrange things without making anything permanent.

We doubled our throughput, which cut passenger wait times in half without adding anything besides space and information. There were no recurring costs, and as with any governmental agency, it was important not to keep requesting more funds. We managed our budget well. And the CMU study? It was a class project and didn't cost us anything. Your tax dollars were put to good use.

We looked at the issue closely to determine where the problem rested. To this day, passengers are the greatest holdup in going through a security checkpoint. The efforts to improve their engagement to expedite screening continue.

In the authors' group, my peers and I encounter an infinite number of problems. Many don't cost money to solve. They are only problems in that they are perceptions of problems. I love the quote from Jack Sparrow (*Pirates of the Caribbean*). *"It's not the problem that's the problem. It's your attitude about the problem."*

Almost all problems can be solved once they are broken down into smaller pieces. Solve the small problems, and the big problem won't seem so big. Starts with the definition. Sometimes, solving the big problem makes the small problems go away.

I don't have any other anecdotes about this because everything with a project or an effort is about solving a problem. *I have no plot.* Then write out the plot. *I have no book.* Then write the book. If you work at any job, you are working on problems that your labor is intended to resolve. Simple as that, from flipping burgers to designing the next-generation spaceship. Problems need to be solved. Define exactly what the issue is and then find the answer. It's what leaders do. It's what every human being does.

13

GETTING ON THE SAME PAGE

Desired leadership mindset: ***Have a meeting that matters***

Meetings are the bane of our existence except when they are well run. Meetings are a conversation to determine a way forward. The meeting ends when the decision is made, then the team puts those decisions into practice.

Status meetings aren't action. Never confuse them with something productive. Status meetings are a testament to the boss not trusting their people enough to read statuses in an email, which reinforces that people won't read the email since you'll beat it to death at a meeting.

Meetings that do not lead to actions are usually a waste of time. I've run my share of useless meetings. I apologize to all attendees for wasting those hours of their lives.

Here are some general tips for a good meeting.

1. Know what decisions need to be made in order to move forward—that is your agenda

2. Make sure the team members have the base information before the meeting

3. Ask questions. Make sure everyone gets their say

4. Consolidate and decide

Every group has meetings—every single one. Anytime you stop to talk about something, that's a meeting. When a sports team calls a time out, that's a meeting. They have thirty seconds to one minute to make their point and adjust what their players are doing. Those are focused and on point.

If you are leading a group of roadside cleanup volunteers, what do you do before you head into the ditch and start bagging trash? Safety check. Make sure everyone is wearing their high-viz vests. Roles and responsibilities. Who is putting the bags by the road for pickup? Who is carrying extra bags, and what happens if you run out? What do you do with heavier trash? How are you going to stay together as you move forward? How long will you be out there? How will you get back to your vehicles? There are a lot of questions for something that might be considered simple, but all of them can be handled quickly.

Get everyone's verbal commitment to their place by having them reiterate what they'll do. That's called the brief-back. It is also an impromptu action confirmation. Remember that meetings are supposed to result in actions. Otherwise, it's just a status update that you could have sent by email.

Back to meetings. They have a greater impact if you get people involved, but as the leader, it's important not to let one person take over the meeting by delivering a *War and Peace*-length diatribe. If you set up the meeting's focus —"We're here to finalize the implementation plan"— anything that takes you off that topic gets tabled for later or never.

"Good points, Bob, but that takes us away from the main purpose of this meeting. Let's table that for a later conversation." And make that a conversation where Bob isn't costing everyone their valuable time, only you. Because your job is to shield your team from the hailstorms so they can get their work done. One on one, you might be able to rein in the conversation to that which is most applicable.

Then you'll have people who occasionally dispute the entire premise of the plan and the actions. If you have covered that ground before, it's apropos to say, "This is not the time. The decision has been made." Take the ball out of their court and press on. It might seem harsh, but if they feel that strongly about it, they can quit. If the person disputing it is your best player, it would make me question why you didn't listen to them earlier in the process.

These are the challenges that you as the leader have to deal with. If you've done the hard work up front—defining the problem your team has to solve and building a good plan that all but one bought into—then you move forward. Sometimes, there's a person who doesn't want to commit, ever.

When those types are in charge, they will find ways to make sure it's someone else's fault if the project goes bad. Non-committal leaders are not the lightning rods their teams need.

When I worked in heavy industry, I went to a plant to do the initial assessment to determine the value of the financial opportunity for process improvements. When I started conducting interviews, I found many employees were defensive and pointed fingers. Fear. They were afraid of being blamed for poor performance.

The first thing I did was incorporate the culture of positive reinforcement and embrace the processes. The lowest-performing individuals improved the most when they realized they weren't going to get punished, only left behind when it came time to give performance awards. The good news was that everyone could get one, and the baseline was their individual performance. We saw big improvements at the plant and a complete change of attitude.

Meetings were better focused, although some rambled on far longer than they should have. But overall, we spent less time in the office and more time in the plant.

In my assessment, I identified a 3.2% opportunity which came out to over a million dollars. After a year, we were able to improve the bottom line by a greater amount, as well as find an expanded market for certain custom products the plant was able to make.

Good people did good work when they were on the same page. Good people found opportunities for the whole plant to do better.

That was a big win. I was proud of that team because it was all them. They only needed to see what they were capable of doing. It was the attitude about the problems and not the problems that were holding them back.

14

THE POWER OF POSITIVE
REINFORCEMENT

Desired leadership mindset: **Positivity improves performance.**
Period.

There are two types of people in the world: those who like
positive reinforcement and those who won't admit they
like it.

What is positive reinforcement? It's a reward to
encourage, at a basic human level, more of the recognized
behavior. It is specific and unique to the receiver. From
something as simple as a look in the eye, a firm handshake,
and a sincere thank you to giving someone an expensive
gift. Positive reinforcement is limited only by your
imagination, but it's important to keep it appropriate to
the level of gratitude, as well as appropriate to the
recipient.

Simple is better when it comes to positive
reinforcement.

Don't give baseball tickets to someone who is not a fan.
They might have cost you a lot and were important to you,

but if they are not important to the recipient, you've wasted your effort. You won't get what you want, which is more of the behavior you were trying to reinforce.

It works on everyone. Look at what you've seen people do with kids. If the curtain-climbers whine enough, they get the candy bar. This reinforces whining, not the opposite. It is unfortunate that you allowed yourself to reinforce the wrong behavior.

That is why participation trophies don't consistently deliver when it comes to behavior reinforcement. If everyone gets the same reward, its value decreases. If you target positive reinforcement specifically at the good actions you want to see more of, you'll be more likely to get them.

Sincere gratitude costs nothing to give. Sprinkle it everywhere it is deserved. Look for reasons to thank people. "Thank you for reworking that pipe fitting. Now it looks like it grew there." When telling someone thank you, be specific about why.

When I was working in the corporate world, we had a great conversation about recognition for not missing any workdays. The plant manager didn't want to do it because he didn't want to reinforce minimum standards. Coming to work was the base minimum (approved absences notwithstanding).

But there was a benefit in a group award, something the team could only accomplish together.

There is such a thing as negative reinforcement, too. You didn't dry your swimsuit, and it's still wet when you need to wear it again. You're going to think long and hard before putting that thing on. If you touched a live wire and received a nice shock for your trouble, that teaches you not to touch bare wires.

Reinforcement both positive and negative needs to

happen as close to the behavior as possible. You want to subconsciously link the consequence with the action. Did good, got a cookie. It's how dogs are trained, and we should all aspire to be as straight-up and loving as dogs. That's a tangent. Let's get back on track.

If someone holds you down and touches you with the live wire to make you suffer for something you did, that's punishment.

In the Marines, there was a fair bit of punishment when the powers that be thought a Marine needed an attitude adjustment. In the brig, take a stripe, lose a half-month's pay. You're busted. In my case, I was busted from Lance Corporal back to Private First Class, lost a little money, and got locked in my room for a while. The Marines look at it as breaking a wild stallion, but there's a big difference between reining one in and crushing their spirit.

What did I learn from it? Not a damn thing. I learned that bureaucrats were little people who liked to lord their power over others. I think too many times, the military resorts to punishment without exploring other avenues for behavior modification. Once I had the Article 15, Non-Judicial Punishment on my record, it made me a different Marine. In the end, it made me less naïve. I stayed in the Corps and did what I could to protect those who couldn't protect themselves. I vowed not to let that happen again, and I did not use punishment on anyone who worked for me.

Let me ask a couple of questions about punishment. As an adult, how do you feel when you are punished? It's demeaning, even if you think you deserve it.

But how do you feel when others are punished? If you think they deserve it, do you cheer? What if you don't think they deserve to be punished? What does that do to morale?

Good leaders shouldn't have to punish their people. Mediocre leaders should never punish their people. I see punishment as a refuge for weak leaders, who use it to dominate others and bend them to their will. That's not the world of today. People have grown smarter and better. This is the twenty-first century. Join the modern world by helping people understand where the team is going, and they will join you because they believe in your vision.

That doesn't mean you don't let people go. There are times when you have to. That's not punishment. That's reshaping your team and a completely different issue. Keep reading.

15

_____

A CANCER

*Desired leadership mindset: **Is the person a cancer, or are you trying to take a shortcut?***

Every team has a naysayer, always negative. They bring morale down. When is the right time to let them go?

This is the hardest conversation a leader will have. Winnie the Pooh always invited Eeyore along despite the dark cloud he carried with him. The group didn't let him dampen their spirits, but imagine what they did for his. Even if he didn't show it.

The easy answer is to let them go, but how will the rest of the team handle that? Will they fear that they are next? They may not have the negative opinion of that person you do.

You have to ask yourself, did you do all you could to change their attitude and bring them into the fold? Be honest since the truth hurts. We tend to shy away from negative people. No one needs that when they're under pressure to deliver. We need an environment in which we can flourish.

You're the leader. You're the one who has to create that environment.

Firing people because they aren't sufficiently positive is bad form. Firing people for actively trying to undermine the team? That's a different issue.

I've had to do it, and it sucks. But when the person truly is a cancer, after they're gone, you'll see a marked improvement in the team. Just like a doctor removing a tumor—once it's out, no one needs to talk about it anymore. It's about the health of the patient, just like it was from the beginning. Same with a toxic individual—it's about the health of the team from start to finish.

Do it right and you win. Do it wrong, and you'll create a crack worse than what you thought you were fixing. So, how do you do it right?

Have a conversation where it's not about the individual but about the behaviors that aren't working for you. Tell that individual what you want and what you don't want. I'm not talking about "I want you to stop being a jerk." You can think that, but name-calling won't get you what you want. If they are underperforming on their job and creating more work for others, it requires conversations about expectations.

They have to meet certain standards. You have to ask yourself whether you helped them understand what all that meant and set them up to win.

The gotcha is something toxic people may try to use on you.

"The project plan is straightforward, and we agreed to it. It doesn't help to have someone saying that it's stupid and won't work. What would help is hearing why you think that with details so we can mitigate those concerns. We'll do what it takes to move forward."

Shaping a discussion in this manner is the best way to reduce conflict. The devil is in the details. What are the points that need to be addressed? Go after them. Clarify them or fix them. There is probably something you overlooked, even if it was as simple as the individual's role in the project.

Is that nebulous enough for you? I went to a three-day course that was designed to address how to have this conversation, and it was so long and so varied that I found the information unusable. The keys are to find the right questions ahead of time and then work with the other person to answer them.

What is the concern?

What do you (the leader) want?

What don't you (the leader) want?

What is a shared path forward?

You'll expend a great deal of emotional energy worrying about this and preparing for the conversation. It will distract you until you sit down and talk, and talking is what needs to happen, with both people getting their share of the conversation. If the person doesn't feel like they're being listened to, you will make no progress.

Remember my first point back at the beginning of this book? *This isn't about you. This is about your shared project.* Even if it's just a Facebook group. You still have a shared goal you are trying to reach.

One of the worst things you can do is to schedule a meeting. "I need to talk with you in my office tomorrow morning." Go to the Kiss of Death chapter and see how you've just undermined yourself to the point that you might not recover.

You've just given this other person a great deal of unnecessary anxiety. They'll think the worst possible thing. You will have a hard time recovering from making a person on your team suffer, even if it wasn't your intent. So don't do it. Settle it as soon as it becomes an issue, then settle it some more until you are both sure it's settled.

Fill the information void with something good.

Give it your best shot before deciding the cancer will only grow and needs to be cut out.

There is no coming back from kicking someone out. No number of apologies can make it better.

When removing people becomes easy, you need to remove yourself, too. You will have failed everyone who was counting on you to lead them. Give the hard people a fair share of your time. You need to make the time, and this is where the glamor of being in charge loses its luster. You work long hours, but people are counting on you.

Then there are those who seem to be actively working against you.

Put yourself in their shoes and try to understand how they see it. Empathy will help you over many hurdles. You can't be in a hurry with this, even if you're up against a deadline.

That makes it even more important to have that conversation early, as soon as it seems like there will be a problem.

See how I've circled back? Unleash the leader within and bring everyone on the team along. Helping someone get past their negativity to become a valuable member of the project will earn you more bonus points than any number of baseball tickets.

Because it's not about you. It's about the project and keeping the team moving forward until they complete it.

You can't buy loyalty, but once you've earned it, keep earning it.

When they win, you win. That is what good leadership is about.

16

THE KISS OF DEATH

Desired leadership mindset: ***Don't let rage seize you in its ugly grasp***

Say your emotions get the best of you, and you start demeaning your team. What do you do now?

Step aside because you're done. You *never* get to do this. Praise in public, punish in private. That saying has a lot of merit, not that punishment is a good leadership tool. You should avoid using it. Corrective actions are more likely to help make a difference. Punishment stops behaviors—all of them. If you have to punish someone, you need to have a serious talk privately, because worse problems might be coming. Public excoriations are like self-inflicted floggings. They only reflect poorly on the leader.

They are the kiss of death.

Shine a light on the behavior that's not helping the individual and the team, then work with that individual to change the behavior. Once again, do it privately. Don't have those conversations in public.

There were times in my career when I wasn't easy to work with. The best leaders, those who deserved all the respect, would pull me aside and do exactly what I describe above. "Your actions are taking us down the wrong road. Here's what I need you to do and why." We stood side by side to look at the goal together, then we'd step off afresh.

Leaders don't get to melt down. Put on a strong face, even if you don't feel it.

You'll thank yourself later, and if it gets worse, get some outside help to talk you down off your ledge.

The worst thing you can do for your team's morale is have an emotional outburst. It could be difficult to recover from.

Trust is hard-earned but easy to lose. Once it's gone, you'll have a hard time getting it back. You're the leader. You must be the one they look up to when it seems like nothing is working. Lighthouses don't get to quit working when the storm is at its worst since that's when they are needed the most.

The light shines just as bright during the daytime, but there's a lot of other light sharing the day. The darkness is when your light matters.

But if you've crashed your people on the rocks, everything was for naught.

Keep your cool.

Now, a little louder to reinforce this point. *KEEP YOUR EMOTIONS UNDER CONTROL.*

Leading with emotions is a losing proposition. You can't be all energy all the time. It's easier on your body and your soul to remain focused on the mission without getting lost in emotional turbulence. Your people will feel it. They might lose it. They might be giddy with success.

I can't emphasize this enough. You never get to become

unhinged if you're in charge. If you need to vent and yell, do it with a trusted friend. Don't do it with your team.

Support them. Help them to get back on track if they've lost their way. Cheer with them when they're happy.

But never lose sight of your goal. If you can't see the goal, no one else will either.

Be the leader, calm in the face of fire.

Being passionate is a lot different from leading with emotions. Self-control is the difference. Passion can be focused because you are in charge of how you bring that passion to your efforts.

When I'm feeling down, I don't wallow. I give something away to fans or colleagues. The older I get, the more I realize that having stuff is a pain. It's better to have less. I give away "treasures" from my past. I have cool stuff, at least in my mind. And it's okay if it goes to someone who can appreciate it, even if only for a short while.

I do giveaways for readers of my books, but I saw this employed by a department head in a major production facility. He gave out raffle tickets to his project managers before we started the weekly staff meeting, and then at the end, he'd draw a number. The winner received something from his garage. He had a lot of stuff and was trying to draw down, one gift at a time. We had great fun. He always remained stalwart no matter what was going on.

He was a man I respect to this day.

We were partnered for a golf tournament, and we won. That didn't hurt either because both of us remained unperturbed under pressure. There was no pressure. We were on a golf course instead of at work.

We earned the respect of our peers that day, too. It was a good time. Take nothing for granted. Be grateful for what you have. And don't lose your cool.

There's too much at stake.

When I worked for the Department of Homeland Security, they hired too many people. They saddled us with seven hundred and fifty employees. We put them to work and did the job, then the headquarters in DC told us the bad news. We were overstaffed and needed to right-size the operation to three hundred and forty-eight.

"Right-size." We embraced the term, but there was no getting around what it meant. More than half our workforce had to go, and those people, the unelected bureaucrats, put it all in our laps. Their problem became our problem with a single memo.

We had a town hall with all the employees to make the announcement. It didn't go well because the bureaucrats from DC didn't have to deal with the pushback. They dropped the bomb and left.

We implemented a number of initiatives. We built a roving team to help those airports that were terminally short. We helped people with their resumes. We encouraged people to look for other work while there was still time so there wouldn't be a gap in their pay. Then we implemented the one-and-done policy. Any rules infraction was a firing offense.

We were given no other choice, and they made me deliver the bad news. Human Resources put me in that bind and left the entire burden on my shoulders. I became known to the workforce as the Angel of Death. I spent my last six months in that job in my office instead of out with the workforce. I was put in a position where no one could win. Performance wasn't good, morale was garbage, and we were putting people in the hospital from the extreme levels of stress, including me. They didn't carry me out of the airport, but I did get carried into the emergency room.

I am still bitter about that, even though it happened a long time ago. The right answer when I could no longer protect my people would have been for me to resign six months before I did. The end was inevitable.

The information void. It's keeping the demons out of your people's faces unless there is bad news, and then it's about delivering it in the best possible way. When I failed to do that, I was finished. I had not failed before, and that was why I hung on, but it wasn't expedient for the government. They made us responsible for their mistake and then made us pay for it.

That was when the employer became the cancer, and I excised myself. I could no longer be effective.

17

FILLING AN INFORMATION VOID

Desired leadership mindset: **Don't allow a void to exist**

When there is a lack of information, people will fill that void with the worst-case scenario until they can speculate to an even greater extreme. They'll embrace the worst thing they can imagine as if it's truth.

This is the axiom I've lived my life by. *Tell people everything you know as soon as you know it.* Keeping secrets doesn't turn out well.

Also, doing what you say you're going to do is the only way to build trust. Trust will always be fragile. I talk about that a lot in this book. You have to trust your leaders. You have to be trusted to be an effective leader.

I always try to tell people what I know, but I have set the personal standard that I don't comment on rumors. I don't have to disprove a negative, but I can say what things *are*.

In heavy industry, it was impending layoffs. It was cost-cutting measures (it seemed like those rippled through the company about once a year). It was too many rumors to be addressed, so we attended the crew briefs every morning. Everyone on the leadership team got out there. They'd talk about what was going on and be honest. If there was going to be a cost-cutting initiative, that came from the top to the whole company within a few hours of when the senior leadership was informed.

By being consistent with the information flow, trust in the message grew, and the rumormongers lost credibility. Those who loved negative rumors always had a small clique that listened, but it didn't infect the company, and people didn't waste a lot of time thinking about the rumors.

What is the best way to cut costs? Ask the people working on the front lines. They can show you where there's waste. By keeping them engaged in the production conversation, you'll stay in a position to run a smooth operation.

Make information-sharing an everyday event. Give your people a place to see or hear the latest information. Avoid ambiguity because human beings have a tendency to select the worse of two interpretations.

Some will select an option that doesn't exist and embrace it like they're drowning and holding onto a life preserver. Understand that will happen. All you can do is your best.

The biggest challenge is not speculating when your people ask pointed questions. If you don't know, tell them. If you do know but can't tell them, then tell them what it's not. Reduce the risk of the black hole swirling around your team.

Then make sure they have plenty to keep them busy. Idle hands and all that. You still have a job to do and goals to reach.

Drama. If we could have a single day without a manufactured controversy or another source of outrage, that would be a pretty good day. You can make your own choice about being happy or not. Don't get sucked into the black hole. Drama will waste more company time than anything else. Whether it is from the rumormonger or two employees saying mean things about each other, there will always be something.

Always.

Keep your eye on the ball, to use a sports metaphor. Watch it all the way into your hands to make sure you catch it. Keep your team focused on that and away from the perception of an information void to save yourself the time and grief of dealing with the aftermath of misinformation.

As the project grows, it will seem like you are always talking, rehashing the same information. Sometimes you have to. Make sure everyone maintains a single base of knowledge. That reduces the variety of interpretations, which shrinks the information void.

Consistency is the armor that protects the project.

On a side note, it's okay to say "I don't know." If it's important for the project, then it's better to say, "I don't know, but I'll find out."

Keep the void filled and your people working toward the goal.

18

A LEADER'S TOUCH

*Desired leadership mindset: **Understand your reach***

In the military, we looked at this as "sphere of control" and "sphere of influence." A leader had direct control over three to five people. That was it. These are the people who get the message first and understand it the best. They pass it down the chain. Pretty soon, everyone has gotten the word.

Understand your role in your organization. There are corporate leaders who think they have direct control over twenty, thirty, even one hundred people. And by control, I mean personal engagement where you understand each other at a foundational level. I don't mean robotic compliance with commands.

That's not possible because you cannot carry on a direct and candid conversation with that many people. There isn't enough time in the day. If you are broadcasting your message, that's sphere of influence, not control. It's the difference between a pyramidal hierarchy and a flat one. In a flat organization, everyone gets the message at the same time.

What if one person has a problem? You go deal with it. What if three people have problems? They will multiply if there is no one else to handle them. I am a fan of pyramidal hierarchies because the ability to handle problems trickles down as well as gets filtered coming up the chain. By the time the issue gets to the top, there should be plenty of input on how to resolve it.

Ask questions. Listen to the answers. Maintain the vision. This is you, the leader at your very best, leading, and if you have to, making the decision and moving forward.

Put the project before yourself. If you have a flat hierarchy, how do you problem-solve? Find the specialists, the ones with the answer. Get out there and canvass the group. This is where a flat hierarchy breaks down. If you think you can do it all by email or message, you lose that personal touch, and your efforts fall into the realm of sphere of influence and out of your direct control.

It's important to understand how far you can reach out and touch people. It's also important not to sell yourself short on your sphere of influence. In the writing group, I can send a message to ten thousand people at a time. It is a great thing that we can do with modern technology. With Zoom and social media videos, we can touch a lot of people at once and have a recurring impact as people watch our message at a time that's more convenient to them. It's the twenty-first century, and messages are stored forever.

Even if you don't want them to be—and that is an important point to keep in mind. When you step into the public eye, nothing is ever off the record. When you make a video, even if you delete it, there will be a copy out there somewhere. The worse it is, the more copies there will be.

Leading is about delivering the right message in the right way. When you talk to an audience and not your inner circle, make sure you don't let your hair down. Be the person they need you to be.

That's what your inner circle is for—those three to five people who are closest to you and are helping you.

Reality says that five people will be plenty taxing, and they are the extent of how far you want to reach before you start shorting everyone on time and effort.

Stay in control, most especially of yourself.

19

CHAMPIONS

Desired leadership mindset: **It's not who you are but who you are surrounded by**

From superhero to supervillain, they stayed in power because they were influential. They convinced their followers of the right path ahead. In the comics and graphic novels, we find supervillains surrounded by henchmen while the hero acts alone.

That's not how it is in the real world. Any successful person is surrounded by those who make him or her better. Period.

"Hey! If it weren't for me…"

Hold that thought. Remember when I started with the leadership premise that it wasn't about you, even though you are the lighthouse keeping the ships from crashing on the rocks? You are the glue holding the team together. You are running around trying to be all things to all people. Without you, this project might have died a quick and ugly death.

You helped people make critical contributions to keep the project moving forward, but you needed the people who were implementing the plan. You needed them to buy into your vision. You aren't a team without a team.

How can I relate that to being a self-published author? You needed your editor to give you her best effort. You needed the cover designer to bring perfection to the imagery. And you needed the fans to trust you to bring a good story. Without your support team delivering for you, there might not be a book, or it would only be a pale imitation of what it would have been with a good team supporting you.

And your author peers. As you grow, your peer group will grow until you find yourself having casual conversations with international bestselling authors. Because they were once like you.

You are paying many of them to produce something for you. So what? You've never been let down by something you paid for? You've never seen workers at a day job giving less than their best effort? The real world is a miasma of emotional turmoil that often prevents people from working hard at what they've committed to. Way too often.

This where you as the leader give them something greater than themselves to believe in. It's an opportunity for them to tune out of their everyday concerns and work toward something they can embrace and be happy to be a part of.

From fans to loyal companions. Do right by them, and they'll do right by you.

Every leader needs their champions. Even in the Marine Corps. I deployed with people I wouldn't follow to the bathroom. Needless to say, those exercises suffered. The difference between the Marines and other places was that when the heat was on and things got real, everyone rose to the occasion. That didn't mean the lieutenant wasn't trying to get us killed, but that was when the gunnery sergeant pulled him aside to save him from himself. Because we had good people.

He didn't treat us like that, though, and he was hands-off too much. When he was hands-on, it wasn't good either. That highlights the point that leadership isn't something you turn on and off. Be present.

Leaders stand apart while also standing with their teams.

In the Marine Corps, it's called leading from the front. The first into battle. The first to face the enemy.

The rest of the time, leadership doesn't involve your imminent death, and I hope it never does. But if the threat is that significant, leadership is more important than ever because a good leader will give hope.

Everything I've put in this book applies. Leadership principles are universal.

20

FIVE STAGES OF DISBELIEF

Desired leadership mindset: **Embrace your doubt**

This is a very specific discussion about publishing a book, but if you look closely, you'll see that it parallels any new project. The track of self-publishing, also called the Five Stages of Disbelief.

Which are healthy, by the way. We learn more from our mistakes than we do from our successes. Those who hit it big with their first book when they have no idea what they are doing are hard-pressed to replicate that success. Mine was a slow build to success. Took lots of books and adjustments over time to build an audience and keep them coming back. There are two tracks—a failure track and a success track—and they look identical. I believe you learn more from the failure track if you remain focused on a long-term goal.

Stage 1: FEAR. It is the moment you hit publish and wonder how your book will be received. Strangers reading your book and judging you by it.

Stage 2: SOCIAL PROOF. From the pit of despair to the peak of joy, you will dip and rise like waves crossing an angry ocean. The first review where someone liked your book. The first review where someone didn't. Sales! The dip to no sales. You will be paralyzed by trying to produce the next book. You'll watch closely, waiting, wondering.

Stage 3: ANALYSIS. What did I do right? More importantly, what did I do wrong? Input. Who do I listen to? What next?

Stage 4: RELUCTANT FOCUS. You start putting together your plan for the next story, but there is a nagging in the back of your mind. You go back and forth between stages 2 and 3, looking for clues on how to adjust your next book. The writing? The covers? The hook? The marketing? Where is it lacking, and more importantly, what do you do about it? This is the key stage for long-term success.

Stage 5: MOVING FORWARD. If you have embraced failure, this is where you stop. You believe you're not good enough. You may not be—*yet*. Take the lessons and try something different. If you don't write another book, you will fail. For those who had unmitigated success, plow ahead! Have you learned the right lessons to make the next even better? Get it done, and you're back to FEAR. Two might not be as good as one. In fact, it might be bad. How harsh a blow will that be? Did you let your ego get the best of your good sense? "I know this is small to some, but I made $10,000 my first month!" What if you make $1000 your second and nothing your third?

Overconfidence is just as destructive as underconfidence. I believe everyone has a great story in them, a wealth of knowledge that is unique to them. Sharing that through a story or a non-fiction title is not intuitive. It takes practice with an eye toward self-improvement, which means you can't keep writing in a vacuum. That's more of the same, and it will get you the same result. One book with no sales will be twenty books with no sales if you don't do something different. Who do you listen to?

The fans. The readers you think will most like your books. Sometimes you get it wrong—those aren't your readers, but other genres might be. Once you find the right group, listen to them, but in a way where it's still you telling the story. Read books to fill the gaps in your knowledge. Are you going to be a professional? Then do what professionals do and study your trade.

There is a low bar to entry in becoming a self-published author. The bar gets higher the farther you progress in your career. No one will love you until they do. Most of the time, they don't know you are there. Finding them is only a small part of the battle. If you've found them but they don't buy, what next? What went wrong? Stage 3—ANALYSIS. Put on your business hat and see what it takes to sell this product.

But I only want to write! If so, prepare yourself to be in a constant state of unhappiness. Would you rather be unhappy for a few hours here and there while doing the business stuff to realize the joy of being a successful author? 20Booksto50k® shows you that the business stuff isn't bad. If you can write a book, you can learn the other things you need to know to sell it. Assume your first book could be better but get it out there because you'll be the worst judge of whether it is good or not.

Keep learning. Keep moving forward. Take control of your destiny. Would you rather be driving your vehicle where you want to go or let someone else do the driving?

I'd rather be in the driver's seat. It's where professionals sit.

21

SELF-CARE

Desired leadership mindset: **You can't help others if you self-destruct**

Eschewing yourself doesn't mean you don't matter. It means you don't put yourself at the top of the accolades pile. It also means you don't get to vent like others without worrying about repercussions.

Eat well, sleep the right amount, and stay as fit as possible. Too many cast off everything else when they are in charge, leaving their bodies as mere shells of their former selves. I don't work out enough, but I avoid most junk food and processed sugar.

There are a large number of books and online forums to better your physical condition. You don't have to look like an underwear model; you only need to provide your brain the right amount of energy to keep your wits about you. When you are weak and tired, you'll start making mistakes.

Understand what it takes for you to be at your best and

then push those boundaries just a little. If you start working twenty-hour days, you'll quickly find your physical health degenerating. The last thing you want to do is keel over when the team needs you most.

No matter how fervent the pace, take breaks and give yourself enough downtime to recover your energy. Five or ten minutes an hour—whatever you can take to get back into the fight with a fresh mind and a fresh body.

Because you matter. You have to make sure your people take their breaks, too. At the end of the day, go home. Sometimes you can take work with you, but don't make it a habit unless that's what you've always done.

Your thoughts become your words which become your actions which become your habits. Habits are how you set yourself up to succeed or fail. Make sure you embrace the right actions to develop the best habits. "We take ten minutes an hour. Get some water, walk around a little, hit the restroom, and come back ready to go." Your words. Let them lead to good habits for both you and the team.

I like to call the body a meat wagon for your brain. Treat it well so it can triumphantly carry your head around. As much as we like a strong body, it's the mind that says the words and plans the actions. It is the mind that drives the process forward.

In Northwestern's Kellogg School of Management's senior executive intensive training course, physical fitness is a key aspect. Each day starts in the gym. Work hard if you want to work hard.

Simple as that. Taking your physical health into account when assuming a leadership role is a key factor in helping you and your team realize success.

22

HUMILITY OF INDIVIDUALITY

Desired leadership mindset: ***You can always improve***

Self-improvement is a forever journey. There can be no point in a leader's life where you think you're good enough that you don't have to work at it. You could shape your words better. You could anticipate the questions and answer them before they come. You could put your people more at ease.

There are so many things that can be done better. The good news is that those on your team will be forgiving if they see you doing better with each new day.

All it takes to be "better" is one small step at a time. The big scheme of life is infinite in its scope. You will never be "the most better." It's important to embrace the mindset that you can always improve and keep striving toward it.

Each night, I sit and review what I did during the day, where I upset myself with blurting incongenial words or taking less than admirable actions. I catalog it in my mind to keep a running tally. There have been fewer and fewer over the years, and what concerns me now is far less than what bothered me when I was younger.

I still have a long way to go because this is about the journey. There is no ultimate destination for a leader. You will always have people look up to you in that role. Are you doing right by them and the project? Most importantly, are you doing right by yourself?

As soon as you start thinking you're the cat's meow, it's the beginning of your downfall. It's time to regroup and challenge yourself and your team in a better way. Success on one mission is just that—a single data point. A foundation on which the rest is built.

Don't let it be the sum total of your achievements.

You didn't peak in high school. You had your whole adult life in front of you.

It's time to make a difference in more lives than just yours. That is the point of this book. It's not about you while being all about you.

Your journey is yours alone while supporting and being supported by your team. Dichotomies abound. Sometimes you'll feel like you're carrying your teammates on your shoulders. You'll feel like you're the one doing all the work. And you might be.

That is where you need to find ways for the team to contribute without becoming dictatorial. It's the learning process of leading. It comes back to you. It's still about you. Where did you fail when it came to building the team, delivering the vision, or guiding the process as the team moved through inch stones toward the goal?

Humility of individuality. If you can't run, walk. If you can't walk, crawl. If you can't crawl, find someone to carry you. That might be what your team has done. You carry them until you find a way for your team to crawl, then walk, and ultimately run.

This is your chance to do better. To be better. Right up to your last day.

23

MEANT TO BE

Desired leadership mindset: **Embrace the role. Enjoy the ride.**

Being the leader in a big project isn't for everyone. It's not something you can jump into without ever having managed something before.

We teach the ins, outs, and jiggly bits to our fellow authors in the 20Booksto50k® group. If you can write a book, you can do all the other stuff, but you won't know that until you do it.

It's the same no matter what industry you're in. People generally work their way into leadership positions. Many times, it's well-earned. Others, it's a mystery why one person was selected over another. Have you ever seen a good co-worker move into a new role and all of a sudden, they aren't doing well?

Leadership is a different skill set, but one you can learn when you understand the basic principles I've put into this book. There's a wealth of doing the wrong things that ended up in here as the right stuff to do. My adult life would have been much better had I known then what I know now.

It's never like that, though. I'm a science fiction author, so I understand that we can only move forward in time. You can never go back except when you learn how to keep moving forward.

The greater good. Your people are the ones who will make it happen. Eschew yourself.

So many ways to misstep as a leader, but sincerity, humility, and honesty are things no one can take away from you. If you've done right by your people, they will be more forgiving and help you help them.

The process of nurturing delivers a greater yield to you, to your team, and ultimately, to a successfully completed project.

Even if the project is as simple as fixing a leaky faucet or as great as building a nuclear-powered aircraft carrier. Inspire, inform, and be greater than what you imagine. The power is in those who follow. Can the leader bring out the best in them?

That is where the greatest leaders come from. They come from within when you deliver a vision that's worthy. Help establish individual goals that build to the team goal. Help your people realize the best within themselves.

For the team and beyond.

Bring out the leader within. We all have it inside us if only we remember one thing. It's not about us while being all about us.

24

MESSAGES

A crisis is a window into one's soul. My job in 2020 was to write books. Those books paid me. I also saw my job as bringing order to a chaotic world. I am compelled to give back to a world that has been kind to me. And I did. When the chips were down, I wasn't. I kept steering the boat. This section shows how I communicated with our author group and the messages I shared outside of the daily one-hour talk show I ran. Anything and everything to keep them from thinking about their problems and get them back to managing their businesses. *The business of being a self-published author.*

"The mind is everything. What you think, you become." **Buddha**

Back in March when the lockdowns started happening and warning flares were being sent in all directions, I said this was the kind of crisis that would show people's true nature, a window into their souls. Some handled it well; others did not.

Five months later, there's time to reflect. Can you look at yourself in the mirror? If you can't, forgive yourself and do better tomorrow. There's plenty of crisis left, both perceived and real.

If you can, forgive those who can't. It's the only way we can all move forward. Many have had their lives turned upside and changed forever, usually not in a good way. The sun still rises. It's not the challenges that endure, but how we respond to them.

In the Marine Corps, we used to say, "Embrace the suck." When things were bad, we rolled with the flow, looked for opportunities to extricate ourselves, and fired when the shot was there. It'll come. Be ready for it.

And there you go—mixing the wisdom of Buddha with the wisdom of the Corps. Oorah.

The morass of self-inflicted anxiety

Knowing it's there isn't the same as being able to do something about it. It's like telling your spouse to calm down. That doesn't work. "Take it easy while we get the life preserver to you, but my coffee is getting cold. Just one more drink, then I'll fling the ring your way..."

Control what is in your control. Create your actions based on what you can do to influence your current and future publications. Use what's in your control to influence what you can. But that's all you can do. Many leaders think they can control their people's actions. They can't; they can only influence them. The more they try to control, the less they influence. This is you as a self-published author.

You can never control whether someone buys your book. You can only influence them. You can control writing a good book, a better book, a book that is more to their liking, a book that draws those readers in.

I wrote a book. I thought it was a good book. One reviewer I listened to slammed it because I didn't give a co-protagonist enough horsepower. I agreed and wrote the next book with that in mind. That was a good book, too, but it was the worst-received book in the series. I made one guy happy for one book while losing some influence on the other 90%. Books 8, 9, and 10 in that series made up for it, but out of all ten books, lucky number seven was a dog's breakfast because of letting someone influence my actions and affect my influence on the rest of my team. I recovered, and guess who one-starred number 8 and magnificently flounced? No surprise. Control what's in your control to deliver the best product to the greatest number of readers. That's how you make money. If you're doing it by writing stories you like to write, that's a double win. That's the only way to win over and over.

You control what you write. You control how you react to criticism, feedback, market intelligence (knowing the tropes), and your readership. You control how those words go on the page. If they aren't good, then learn to write better. That's in your control. Even Michelangelo didn't start off painting like Michelangelo—he practiced, he sketched, and he trained. Don't be dissuaded because you've written some righteously appalling, fully compostable words. You get better with a bar to raise over and over.

Are you going to quit because practicing and learning is too hard? Go ahead. Those who don't quit are the ones who find greater traction as they climb, as long as they control what is in their control to influence that which can be.

1 March 2020

.   .   .

Captain's Log: 20Booksto50k(R) is shut down every Sunday and Wednesday for new posts in order to give the admins a break (they are all authors of some repute, ill or otherwise). I'm up to my eyeballs trying to get everything in order from yesterday's hurricane, so let's talk Vegas, because I don't get to think about anything else right now.

This is the biggest indie author convention in the world and I think it is now the biggest author convention out of them all. It is also one of the least expensive and the most accommodating because we focus on one thing. Your words have value and how you can realize that revenue. Nothing else matters—it's amazing what you can accomplish if you keep your eyes on the prize. I run this conference at cost. I make all decisions on who is put on stage before you. I put people up there who are some of the best in their fields to give you the best information possible for you to pick and choose from. We set the buffet and it is completely up to you what you put on your plate. Indies helping indies to help themselves.

And more than 1500 people have paid good money because they believe in this premise and are willing to work hard for themselves and their careers (or secondary income—it's all up to you).

Comment with what you want to get from a professional author's conference (or you can say nice things about past 20Books events).

15 March 2020

Captain's Log: Productive Time

I know you're all browsing Facebook. Go get some words, edit some words, read some words. Think kind thoughts, no matter how awful things may be in your life, or the lives of others. Tomorrow takes care of itself today.

Peace, fellow humans

19 March 2020

Captain's Log: Checking In

I upgraded my chair since I'm going to be in the hotel for a while. Otherwise, I'm as healthy as I'm going to be (I'm high risk and am almost completely isolated from other humans) except for the extra pounds I'm packing on from living the total bachelor lifestyle. I tried to do some sit-ups this morning. That wasn't pretty. But I am getting the words. Looks like a solid 3000 today. I got distracted with a bunch of side tasks that were all about others, so it was time well spent, but didn't add to book length. My wife is perfectly fine, too—she's living the life of Reilly having the house all to herself while in quarantine following her trip to Spain.

What about you? Let us know how you are and maybe a thing or two you're doing for others, even if it is something as simple as making an extra phone call or three. Your extroverted friends are not okay, but we've been training for this our whole lives.

Go forth (within the isolation of your own home) and do great things for others (digitally), while taking good care of yourselves.

Peace, fellow humans.

26 March 2020

. . .

Captain's Log: A $200 grant to take the edge off for someone in dire straits due to the layoffs from COVID-19.

Here's what I've made total from my Successful Indie Author series in March. I'll nearly double that to $1000 and give away $200 to five different folks who are on the edge of going under because of job loss and their books aren't yet earning. Send an email to 20Books@craigmartelle.com with the Subject Line: 20Books Grant Request (your name). I'll need a short note from you about your request, plus a PayPal email address. If you have books published, your author name and maybe a link to one of your titles.

Since there won't be any luncheons this year for obvious reasons, I'll roll the SIA series money back into the members in most need.

EDITED TO ADD: thanks to the overall generosity of the group, we will be able to help out at least twenty people with $200 each, maybe more per request, depending. Such incredibly generous people have jumped in to offer their assistance to group members as well. This has taken off and we now have a bit over $5000 to distribute, so I think we will give a little more than $200/person or extend it to a second month. And this is worldwide. You don't need to be in the US for this. Everyone is suffering, but some more than others. How do we make this transparent? I am humbled that people trust me with their money, but I want everyone to be comfortable that it has gone to a good cause. I don't have this answer because I don't want to name the people we've helped because no one needs to know if you're in a tough position. Many have a tough time asking for help. I will continue to think on this to make sure we protect privacy as well as stay above board.

It's not going to make your mortgage payment for you (but a number of banks are waiving fines/penalties/anything bad for those who miss their mortgage payments, although not all are), but it could make the difference between eating or not. Apply only if you're desperately in need. I'll probably do the same thing next month, too, because a rising tide and all that.

Just promise me to keep working on your words. This isn't a handout. It's a bet that you wouldn't be here if you didn't want to learn about self-publishing. You can't do that if you're starving to death or living on the street.

7 April 2020

Captain's Log: The End

75,800 words in 24 days with a surge of 7385 words today to finish it up. After a last read through of the final couple chapters, I sent it to a dev editor for his review tonight. I'll clean up any major issues tomorrow and send it to the copy editor when it's ready (probably tomorrow—I don't see any major issues appearing).

Every finished book is worth celebrating. I hadn't intended to produce more than six books this year, but this is my fourth of the year already. Not traveling and not expecting to travel has cleared my mind. Being in lockup has helped focus me. The daily C&M Show keeps me motivated to get the stories done.

Drink of choice is water because I'm trying to trim down a bit (take some strain off my heart).

Now it's time to go do something physical—I'll snow-blow my driveway. The winds driving yesterday's snow left drifts. Not that we're going anywhere or anyone is coming. But it'll be something to do that's not too taxing. And I love driving my tractor.

Peace, fellow humans

19 April 2020

. . .

Captain's Log: 20Booksto50k(R) is closed every Wednesday and Sunday to give the admins a break.

It is almost impossible to set anything in place for fall or beyond. I'm going to put Cabo 2021 on ice because the time is not right for that. I need things to happen this summer to set things up and there is no way we can. The Pacifica is currently closed. We'll see what they look like coming out the other side. For the authors who would attend, the worldwide shutdown is probably not affecting us as much as others, but it sends the wrong message to be setting up a Davos-style retreat, when so many people are hurting. Depending on what the new world looks like by the end of summer, I may revisit this. I am still operating under the premise that 20Books Vegas is a go. Sam's Town is going to open ahead of the strip casinos so they'll have their procedures solidified well in advance of us coming.

In the most famous of questions from Spock's human mother, How do you feel? Right now, let's get to the basic foundation of your existence. I'm okay. I'm not okay but am working through it. Maybe it's I'm not okay and I don't know what to do. We're here. Over 39,000 of us working toward realizing the value of our words. And thanks to some incredibly kind and generous people (six more donations in the past two days), we have a few nickels to give out from the 20Books Indie Grant fund for those who find themselves in a tragic financial position. It's not much per person, but hopefully it's enough to keep food on your table to get you over this hurdle. If you would like to be considered for a grant, here's how you do it.

Please send an email to 20Books@craigmartelle.com with the Subject Line: 20Books Grant Request (your name). I'll need a short note from you about your request, plus a PayPal email address. If you have books published, your author name and maybe a link to one of your titles. Also your Facebook name that you are a member of 20Booksto50k(R) with.

You can send donations to craig@craigmartelle.com—I keep a running tally and provide updates here with totals.

3 May 2020

Captain's Log: Road to $500k is filled with potholes:) We'll make it the road to $350k plus. EDITED: The first image I copied in was missing data from quite a few titles.

This month saw a very consistent $700 to $800 per day with the exception of a couple pre-order releases that delivered a twelve hundred dollar day and a thousand dollar day. Total revenue came in a little north of $20k when I add in audio and affiliate. I had no other ancillary revenue streams this month.

My expenses were up a little, but some costs were down. My ads and promotions ran $2k less than what I had budgeted—still $5k spent—$3k on Amazon, $1500 on Facebook, and $500 on promotions (BookBarbarian, ENT, Robin Reads, Bargain/Freebooksy, and a few more).

My co-author shared royalties this month were high because my biggest selling titles in April were co-authored accounting for $5000 in royalty payouts.

My set recurring costs (executive assistant, website, a second helper, and software) came to $1500.

I bought a few covers in April for releases, so that came to an extra $1000.

Total royalties—$20,900

Total expenses—$12,500

Net pocketable profit—$8400 (of which about $2k will go to taxes—next estimated payment is due on June 15).

I am investing more in my ads for May and June by sending a couple folks to training. When they graduate, I'll turn them loose on Facebook ads primarily. I should see a ramp-up in spend along with a corresponding increase in revenue. I consider an ROI of one to one to be a success for their first month without the training wheels. I'll give them a couple grand each to play with and see what they can do with it. We'll review weekly numbers and progress as well as keep the pump primed with ad copy and graphics that they can try.

This is how I spend my money and track it each month. I look at the macro view. I set up two major promotions a month where I increase sales at a decreased price and that helps keep my revenue steady. You'll see the nice tail on the LMBPN published chart—that is my most recent title released last week in my current most popular series. We'll try to keep that tail fat by hitting book one hard on some new FB ads.

These charts are from BookReport. LMBPN is Michael Anderle's publishing company for our co-authored titles. CMI is Craig Martelle, Inc (as a lawyer, I like easy). Blue is page reads and red is revenue from sales. Gray along the bottom is for paperback sales.

3 May 2020

Captain's Log: Practicing what I preach.

I write long series and I promote the first books in series. Here's the first page from my Author Central sales info tab. This is also how you make good money as a Blue Collar author. I don't have any runaway bestsellers here, but a good number of solid performing books (especially first in series and then omnibus editions). The top book on this list is the first story I ever wrote. I sold a total of 53 copies before it was picked up by an imprint of Simon & Schuster, so that one is trad pubbed. I ran a big promo last week and my publisher hit their list and worked a little of their magic to get it up to #55 overall in the store. Don't be impressed. I set up the marketing campaign and paid for all the promos. I more than broke even, but didn't make as much as any of the other books on this list, but I remain one of my publisher's favorites:) They have even promoted two of my self-pubbed titles to their list (post-apoc survival).

The other titles show the result of marketing the first in series and then the power of a complete omnibus edition when I've completed a series. The omni here was consolidated and published more than two years after the series' final book hit, so the individual books were running their course. This juiced the revenue stream big time—the set made it up to #400 overall three months ago when it published (also had a BB Intl Featured Deal with it).

My current most popular series is my space lawyer. We put our ad money (only about $50/day) on the first in series. We hit the latest with an Amazon Ad for about a week or two and then kill that, relying on the first book to sell the series. The ninth book in that series just published and is holding steady (you see how it helped the sales of the first book as people buy into the whole series—nothing sells the first book like the most recent book). This is how you make steady income over time through a balance of backlist, promotions to juice old series, and new books to keep the old fans on board. It's the long game.

Covers and book titles are provided for illustrative purposes only.

Peace, fellow humans

23 May 2020

Captain's Log: You Can Sell a Great Story

Period. It may take a lot of work to find the right readers and only the readers determine if you have told a great story. It doesn't matter if it's a sub-sub-niche genre. It doesn't matter if you write in a style that's different from everyone else.

But you make your job a great deal more difficult if you deviate too far from reader expectations. You want to blow them away, not because you're completely different, but because you're uniquely different.

Want to make some of the hard things (like freaking marketing) easier? Then make sure your covers will attract the right readers. Make sure your copy is clean enough where the technical aspects of your writing don't yank the reader from what could otherwise be a great story. Readers are fickle but also have faith. Don't paralyze yourself thinking your editing isn't perfect. I ran the same manuscript through two different editors, both of whom I trust implicitly. They both found some of the same stuff, they found different big stuff, and then they varied wildly in the little stuff (it appears there is a vast gulf of application when it comes to commas). So perfect? It doesn't exist. Good enough on the technical points. No one gives a flying goat fuck if you use an Oxford comma or not when the readers have become lost in a great story.

Length doesn't matter as long as the story is complete. I published books seven and eight approximately one month apart. Seven was 51k words and eight was 108k. Same series. No one mentioned the length in book seven reviews. One person suggested book eight was too short. It's all relative. Harry Potter book one is 77k words and book seven is 198k.

Even our Velocirapture book (a dirty dino parody) will sell when written well with a compelling narrative and put into the hands of the right people. If you want to buck trends, then do it to the best of your ability, but understand that when you are trying to push a chain uphill, it could be a lot of hard work.

Writing a book is hard enough without handicapping yourself. More of the same, but different, unique, and stories told well.

Being a professional means learning what it's like to be a master at your craft while also having a sound understanding of the business behind helping something to sell. Your seven-figure authors in here are experts in both. Your six-figure authors get it with a great deal of understanding. Your three- and four-figure authors have some stuff to figure out. But even the authors who are at the top of the charts had to start at the bottom and work their way up. They learned, they applied, and they prospered.

Understand what it takes to be a professional author. That means selling your work for a profit. How big a profit is in your hands. Are you doing what you need to do or are you hoping for success? Hope is a lousy plan. Better to invest your time learning the craft, learning the business, and practicing both to improve with each release.

Peace, fellow humans.

28 May 2020

Captain's Log: The End

Every book deserves a celebration. This book was 135k words, the majority of which I wrote in May (113k words this month). This is the final book in a nineteen-book series. The first volume published in December of 2016 was 57k words. The total words for the nineteen books come to nearly 1.5 million words. I think this is my 103rd book, but my 145th publication once you include short stories.

This is also the longest single book I've written. I was ready to be done writing it and the series, but I needed to tie up loose ends and that took a lot of words so it didn't end too abruptly.

My insider team checked it at 10k words and then again at 50k words. They haven't seen the last 80k words. They are looking at it now so I can make any final adjustments before it's due to my editor Sunday evening. They are jonesing for "the rest of the story."

Next up is the last book in another series. I've budgeted one week to write it. I'll probably start this weekend and get a few scenes down. Already have the first 1500 words done. Target is only 25k words. I'll have that finished by the 7th, and then a new venture to deliver something different and better. Not pulp. Something to compete on the world stage. I'm ready for that challenge. We'll see how long it takes to write and rewrite such a book.

Drink of choice is decaf coffee, black.

Peace, fellow humans.

The Black Lives Matter protests were in full force, and we had to shut the group down lest it devolve from the business of being an indie author.

5 June 2020

Captain's Log: 20Booksto50k(R) is Back in Business.

And it is exactly the same as it was before. The world needs 20Booksto50k(R) as a refuge for people trying to find their way in the self-publishing world.

It is far bigger than one person. It is a beacon of hope to many. The group has changed countless lives for the better. The group is international with members from some 140 different nations. The group is a bastion of learning and camaraderie in the business of being a professional author.

Everyone is welcome to join. There are no dues and no

requirement to ever spend a cent for equal access to everything we have. There is equal opportunity for all.

We ask that you refresh yourselves on the rules—they seem extensive, but they are not. Simply look for the reason the rules are in place—they all stem from two foundational elements. No self-promotion and don't be a dick. That's it. The rules get into the details of where one or both lines have been crossed in the past and needed more explicit clarification.

Study what people have done and what you can try for yourself. We help those who help themselves. No one is going to carry you, but someone ahead of you on the climb up the mountain of success is reaching a hand back. Take it. And keep climbing.

We are the rising tide.

12 June 2020

Captain's Log: The Quality of Your Story

- *is independent of the speed at which you wrote it*
- *you may not be the best judge of whether it is good or not*
- *the readers who pay money for your books are the final arbiters with a buy-through rate to your second book as your barometer of the quality of the first*
- *can be improved*

Today on the C&M show we have the purveyors of a new AI review process for your manuscript. You'll meet Marlowe and we'll talk about how a completely unbiased reviewer (it's an AI) can give you actionable feedback on your story to help you shape it toward successful stories in your genre while leaving the unique nature of your tale.

Authors are the absolute best at self-induced hysteria. Stop it and get a neutral opinion if your readers have not already spoken. Don't torpedo your own author career before it gets off the ground.

Keyword—actionable feedback. Indies striving for better. Indies seizing market share because they are earning it.

A rising tide lifts all boats.

23 June 2020

Captain's Log: What do you need from a professional group?

How about one that provides everything at no cost?

Giving back is important to me and that's why I have invested a huge part of my life into this group, but it's wearing me out. Over the past few months, I've been able to write a few books that have been exceptionally well received. I continue to improve my writing craft. I'm embarking on a couple new ventures—a thriller series, an in-person weekend author business retreat called Indie Capstone, and then the 20Books Vegas conferences through 2022.

Understand why you may not see me as much in here. It's okay. I'm still around, but spending less time on Facebook.

Trying to keep up with all the changes is a huge time suck.

We will have a show in Vegas, but what it will look like is anyone's guess. I know there are a great number of people who are okay with the risk of coming because they trust we'll do everything within our power to mitigate as much of that risk as we can and they trust themselves to do the right thing. Like we do in here with the information people share—keeping it to personal experience because nothing beats first-hand knowledge.

While telling all that they have the responsibility. You own all of it. No one else is responsible for your success.

All I can ask is go out and do something for someone else today, and then do it again tomorrow. Control what is in your control. You are the master of your own destiny. Seize it and don't let go.

23 June 2020

Captain's Log: Why do good stories suck?

Are you writing with character driving your story?

We don't talk craft in here because it is so genre-specific and people get torqued about the most trivial things. I ended booting five people for name-calling during the great Oxford Comma debacle of 2018. Calling people names. Because of the Oxford Comma. By all that's holy, stop the madness!

Take charge of your own storytelling.

Take charge of your career and start writing books that people want to read. We did not harp on the quality of story enough when this group first started—we assumed people understood that, but now, I'm going out of my way to make sure that people understand—you must write a good story. It doesn't have to be perfect. It doesn't have to be great, but it must be good and that is determined by your readers. Do they read the book in one sitting and then start jonesing for the next? That's the result good stories get.

26 June 2020

Captain's Log: It's okay to not be okay.

I see many who are struggling. Find one thing to focus on. Prioritize. And then add more when you get that first thing under control.

It usually starts with family. They are your first concern.

There are three states to being healthy—emotional well-being, physical health, and financial health. You don't need to be rich, but you can't be wondering where your next meal is going to come from. You don't need to be able to run a marathon, but you shouldn't have to suffer to do something you just did last week. And your head needs to be on straight, but for you. Everyone's place is a little different. My body is mostly broken but we maintain a fragile peace as long as I don't overdo it.

My water pump stopped pumping water this morning. It bummed me out, but I called the service that takes care of my house. That'll probably be a $1000 I hadn't planned on spending to join the other gross expenses in June. Still, I'm okay on that front. I've cut my ads back and am realigning.

For emotional health, I write. Yesterday was a 5200-word day. Today will probably be closer to 2500. It's all good. Live in that world each day. A thriller. A little different than my usual, but I'm digging it, going for a different word flow and engagement.

"Sheltered?" Jenny leaned close, her nose touching mine. We spent a great deal of time talking that way. It was strangely soothing, yet fiercely intimate.

I'll post separately on 20Books Vegas 2020 and Indie Capstone. The day-to-day changes are twisting me around as decision deadlines loom. I'll do right by everyone, but understand that we must have 20Books Vegas. Like explorers going to the South Pole or climbing Mount Everest. They did it because it was there and the adventures became safer and safer for those who followed. We will lead the way, showing what is possible when we gather for a singular purpose, fellow travelers on the journey of self-publishing.

Take the steps you're capable of taking, no more, no less. Rest your soul and control that which is in your control.

Peace, fellow humans

4 July 2020

Captain's Log: Irrelevance, Irreverence, and Irregardless

Today must be because it already is. Tomorrow will come, inevitably. Plan for tomorrow, but live for today. Learn from the past, but don't dwell, because today is a new day.

I know what I'm doing today. I know what I'm looking at for tomorrow. I know what I'll want to accomplish this coming week. I'll plan, but today is the day that I live for. There is only one today, regardless of the date.

20Booksto50k(R) is about sharing what we've done, the first-hand knowledge from which you can learn, the experience you can gain, without having to trial things on your own.

You're not alone, but the workday and how you manage it are yours. Decide what you must do, then what you'd like to do, then do it. I had one thing that I had to do today. I had it done by 8:30 AM, a complete re-read and edit of the first book in a non-fiction travel series that I'll be publishing. Back to the team for a couple more reworks, then to the editor, then to the proofreaders, and finally to the offset printer for a minimum first run. Those other things are plans, but I did what I had to do.

I have my thriller WIP. I've finished the primary story, but am into the double snapper to extend it by another 20k. I should finish that first round this week, then it'll be a full review and rewrite to refine the flow, the beats, and the engagement—I'll pick up an author.ai review and make sure the tempo and wording highlights are as I want as well as contrast it with other thrillers to better refine my marketing package. That's the plan.

For today, I'll knock out more story—I wrote 4200 words on it yesterday, 25k words in the last week. For the first time ever, my wife liked the plot and characters.

Thank you all for your The End posts and sharing what you've tried on your launches, both successful and not, your improvements, and where you are on your journey. We all take different routes. We all have different goals. Embrace yours and keep moving forward.

Never forget to do a little something for someone else. It will reduce a touch of the world's pain, even some of your pain. Expend more energy on yourself than trying to get others to change. Plan for tomorrow, but live for today.

We rise with the tide, our own tide.

Peace, fellow humans

7 July 2020

Captain's Log: The End

I celebrate them all. This is something like my fifty-eighth solo written book, my hundred and fourth overall, and nearly 150 titles when I include the short stories.

This book is 70k words long. I had anticipated it would be closer to 100k, but with a clipped approach to the prose, it rolled in much shorter. I wrote it in 26 days and that includes a couple rewrites along with a few stops and starts, but a couple long walks and physical labor (sanding our picnic table) helped me work through sticky plot points to satisfy the so-what with details that made sense.

Success can be found in writing every day. I have a musical score that goes with my book. I shall solicit the band for use of their lyrics (I do not have any within, but I would like to put in a couple stanzas here and there from six different songs—I will get approval and add them or not and leave it as is, just the album and song title).

I have my award-nominated narrator hired for concurrent audio release—he'll record and upload in October. I'll release the book somewhere between Thanksgiving and Christmas with the second book on pre-order (with the available link) immediately after The End.

I will have the paperback with KDP print, exclusive for the 40% royalty and with Ingram for wide distribution, along with the hardback version. I'll release the paperbacks when they are ready to send to a number of readers before the ebook and audio go live.

All of this will be under a Stuart Bache cover.

I will let this manuscript sit for a few days as I need to write a science fiction short story. And then I'll come back for a complete re-read and rewrite to ensure the flow is correct and if there are any places that slow down, I will fix those. As Harlan Ellison said, leave out the parts that the readers don't read. And then I'll reread it once more. After that many re-reads, I'll send it to my beta readers for their read through. I expect the puritans to blush at a few of the scenes, but not put the book down. After that, I'll send it to my editor for the copy-edit. Then to a team of 10 to 20 proofreaders to make sure it reads well. And then it will be ready—this should be mid-August and that's when I'll get the paper and hardback versions going.

That's my plan for this book—the second title in the thriller genre for me, but this one is about vigilante justice, a thriller with a love story and an eye toward a better future. This is a good story that should resonate across a broad band of reader tastes. I'll build my marketing campaign over the next couple months and set the wheels in motion once I pick a release date. I'll spend for a big launch with a follow-up push between Christmas and New Year's.

And that's my plan. The picture is of my 4imprint steel Yeti mug which is now my new preferred coffee receptacle as it puts the least amount of pressure on my arthritic knuckles, unlike a regular coffee (14-oz, it's coffee, not a snifter of brandy) cup. So there we are. My 20Books lanyard collection in the background along with a numbered litho of the Crowning of Charlemagne (Charles Magnus, the grandson of Charles Martel).

24 July 2020

Captain's Log: The Veracity of Truth and the Destruction of Drama

Just to be clear, this group is focused on the business of being a self-published author.

It's important to work hard at the right things—rarely does someone deliver a great novel on their first attempt. Can an author replicate that success? Many cannot. Most have to work their way up. Grinding forward. Learning to write better and better. Learning to market.

It took thirteen books before I hit my first five-figure month (six books in one series, four books in a second, two books in a follow-on series, and one standalone). It took nineteen books before I hit six figures in a year. I hit the second six at twenty-three books.

Focus effort on what works.

Watching other people to learn is good while watching those others to criticize is not. Wasting time tearing others down is toxic to your business for the simple fact that it doesn't make you any better. Only you can improve yourself. Only you are responsible for your success. Be part of the rising tide. Don't be anchored to the bottom while the tide rises around you.

The success stories in here are amazing—from something as simple as getting charged by BookReport because you're making too much money for their free version. Or your first 1000 page reads, first five-star review by a stranger. First royalties. Buying a vehicle. Maybe even paying off your mortgage.

Because readers are willing to pay to read your stories. That is what success looks like for those who want to realize value from their words. Everyone's mountain is different and everyone's signposts on the way up are unique. Keep climbing. Keep rising.

There are good people in this business, a lot of good people. Remove the toxic people from your life, and you'll be amazed at what you can accomplish. Keep focused on your goal. Learn what you need to know when you need to know it. There is way too much to know it all before you start. I have around 140 publications, and I don't know a lot. It's okay. I make do while asking for help when I don't know. Like an upcoming picture book that I'll be publishing to Amazon—never uploaded one like that before. The file is 80Mb. I'll have to do something different to bring it online. There is a process for those and good people in here who have done it.

So many good people out there. They are the tide.

Do great things for yourself while also lifting another up. We make the world we want through our actions and through our words. Make them all count.

Peace, fellow humans.

26 July 2020

Captain's Log: 20Booksto50k(R) is closed every Sunday and Wednesday to give the admins a break.

I accept the premise that most authors are introverts. As such, have you forgiven yourself for that one thing you did twenty or even forty years ago? No one remembers it but you but that remorse is still there, nagging at the back of your mind. Only you can let it go. Be sad. Be angry. Forgive yourself and be better.

Celebrate success. What is the one thing you've done for yourself this past week? Not selfish but self-care. I finally escaped my house for a walk around the neighborhood to burn some calories and work the body. I also cleaned up my hand weights for daily curls. I had to remove weight from them. One only gets weaker without exercise. That goes for the mind, too. Self-care. Thank yourself for another day on this side of the big blue orb. Embrace the world of your story. Teach or entertain or both. Let your words help others.

Peace, fellow humans

29 July 2020

Captain's Log: 20Books 2021

I've had an absolute gullet-full of being stuck in my house. I'm thinking Madrid in June 2021 for a weeklong conference (assuming there's a vaccine and people aren't in constant fear of dying from something they can't see). A weekend conference followed by a five-day writing retreat.

Climate suggests the weather will be a good 60s-80s. Plenty of facilities are available. It's Madrid, so it could be a bit spendy, but you'll be able to Airbnb or stay with friends or rent a caravan or who knows all the ways to save buckaroonies. I have no idea on the cost of the conference—all depends on what the venue would charge us. We'll be frugal because we only charge what we spend.

But Spain, because my wife and I will probably spend a month there next year, assuming we aren't at a Soylent Green level of society by then. Anything better than that, we got businesses to run and words to write. Do we have enough interest *for next year (assuming the world not dying from Capt Tripps and all that)?*

30 July 2020

Captain's Log: Seeing A Greater Life

Bear with me (not bare, keep your clothes on, even if they're jammies).

A decade ago, I was in a Cracker Barrel for a business breakfast with our team. I didn't want to be there. I didn't want to have the conversation that was inevitable. After getting my massive omelet, I asked for Tabasco Sauce. The server said they had Cholula sauce. I replied with "That stuff is terrible." That made me feel terrible and I remember it vividly to this day. How about, "No, thank you. I prefer Tabasco." A simple twist, but one that was a step too far back then—I wasn't happy and took it out on anyone near me. It wasn't their fault.

That brings us to the present day. I may have stressed my body a little too much last year, but thanks to modern technology most of the damage was reparable when they shoved electrodes into my heart and zapped the offending nerves. My breathing is no better, but as long as the ticker is ticking, we'll call it good. I have time before I reply nowadays and do my best to keep it as positive as possible.

I didn't realize what a lifeline 20Books Madrid would be, but it has been and in such a good way, too. We'll start checking venues this week to see what may be available next year for the dates we want at the price we want to pay. I'll plan for 200, scalable to 500. I think we need to start now because once a vaccine is announced and becomes widely available, people are going to flood back to conferences and meetings. Humans were never meant to be alone.

So we go to conferences to be with those of like minds and like goals, those who support what others are trying to do. Nine 20Books events later, I've seen these are the most positive and supportive environments you'll find for self-published authors. Last year, a couple different industry providers told me that 20Books Vegas was the most unique event they had ever gone to because everyone was so supportive. In thirty years of industry shows (that the old pros had gone to), there was always the underlying competitive nature among the attendees.

That's what makes us different. We only compete against ourselves. A rising tide lifts us all, if you'll be open to coming along with us. No one has to lose for us to win.

What prompted this? I know we never talk about reviews, but that's what. My 97th one-star review—shows more about the reviewer than my book. Angry at the world. The nearly 6000 five-star reviewers are able to see the positive things around them and the books for what they are—a story, an escape, entertainment.

You don't need to blow smoke up anyone's ass, but you can't fix the world either. You can only change yourself and how you see our big blue marble. See past the pain. You might find flowers growing all around you.

Peace, fellow humans

26 November 2020

Today is that Thursday, the fourth of the month, where Americans celebrate because it's our only Thursday holiday which means Friday is off for many, but not retail workers. They usually get swamped on Black Friday, the biggest in-person sales day of the year in the USA. I used to never go out on Black Friday, but where I live now, it's just another day. We don't have malls or large retail stores up here competing for customers. You go buy what you need and get back home, maybe picking up a burger from the new Sonic on your way, but you don't eat and drive. Our roads are covered in ice because it's the second of our six months of winter. Life is different here.

It's business as usual for us. We don't go anywhere for this holiday, but we do go hog wild cooking because that sets my wife the professor up for the home stretch as there is one full week of classes remaining after the short break and then to finals week. We have plenty of good leftovers and that is why we cook big on Thanksgiving. A 21-pound turkey for the two of us.

I jam to get the last book of the year done because usually we travel somewhere warm over Christmas (remember that six months of winter part?). On December 21st, we have three hours and forty-nine minutes of daylight. Temps could be in the minus twenties Fahrenheit. It's the best time of year not to be here. But this year we will be. I'll get my new WIP done and start the next. I work every day.

And what does this have to do with the business of writing? Plan ahead. Do what you have to do to stay within your best creative zone. Some days are more productive than others but as an indie, you'll think about your business every day. There's always something to do. Temper it and balance what you do and when you do it. Just like preparing a big meal, you ask, when do we want to eat, and then you backward plan to start the dishes at the right time so everything finishes together.

That's your book. Know how long each process takes and give them their due. While one thing is working, you can focus on another. I waited for edits on one book before starting the next. One time. I wasted two weeks not writing. Unconscionable. I can think of two stories at the same time and switch back and forth when I need to. Just like anything, with practice, this becomes easy to the point of being able to work multiple stories on the same day.

As professionals, we aren't out here alone. We are who we're surrounded by. I have a great team in support of me and it is worth far more than anything I might pay. Because I can't do it alone. And I'm thankful for the wonderful minds and opportunities of this group. We are all in this business together.

Peace, fellow humans.

12 December 2020

I've been getting a lot of questions about motivation lately. You've heard this before. It's okay to not be okay. 2020 has been a horrendous year. From a business perspective, I've made more this year than last. I've also given away a lot more because that makes me feel good. We're not giving any Christmas presents this year. Instead, we're making donations in people's names. Simple as that.

The biggest lesson of 2020 has been the decline of material consumption. People have grown to appreciate what we had taken for granted—the ability to be with others, enjoy a big conference with our peers, do readings, visit family. This goes to our business. We're the artisans who entertain, the insiders who educate. We have a greater role to play in a new world. Keep the minds engaged of those who are down.

Experiences are what people miss most and that is what a book provides. It's something to experience, get lost in a story. Learn what there is to learn. And explore the boundaries of their minds.

What does this have to do with motivation? Opportunity. The greater good. The needs of your fellow humans. The needs of your families. You can fill those needs with your words.

No matter your challenges, someone will always have it worse. Their escape is your escape. Get lost in your words even if only for a short while. It's bigger than you, but it's also all about you. No one else will write your words for you. Macrocosm to microcosm. It's all connected.

Motivation is about doing what it takes to get where you're going. Small steps are still steps forward. Any step is a good step, except the one that takes you backward. Visualize where you want to be, even if you can't see the path to get there. Then look from that point to now. You'll see stepping stones. Lots of them. It's okay. Look at those who have gone before you. They've taken the steps. Your goal is achievable. But you have to take the steps. It may take longer than you want, but isn't the end result worth it?

And then you find a new goal and head for that.

What is the best thing about your WIP? Why do you keep plugging away at it?

30 December 2020

Where we started, where we are, and where we're going are different places. We can only change one of those places. You have today to determine where you want to be tomorrow and beyond.

You are responsible for getting yourself there. It's best if "there" is within your control. If your goal is to be a #1 NY Times bestseller, you have to count on a lot that's not in your control. There's a lot of hope and a lot of luck there. How about writing a great book? That is within your control. And it may not be the book you're currently working on. It might be the next one or the story five books from now.

As you continue on your indie journey, look at what you've learned. Apply it and keep learning. You will never know it all. You only need to know enough. Embrace what better looks like and keep striving for better and only you can determine what better looks like for you and your situation. It helps if you have readers that you trust from your genre to make sure that your story resonates.

A great story, as determined by those people who vote with their money.

There is no perfect. There is only good enough and sometimes that means better, maybe the best you've ever written, but is it? You're an artist. Take pride in your work. Are you effectively entertaining and/or educating? If you think that the readers are stupid and don't understand the message you are trying to deliver, you might want to think about how you put the book into the wrong reader's hands. Or how you didn't deliver a message in a palatable way. There's only one person you can control here and that's you. Put it into different readers' hands. And you may find that it's not them.

It's you and you have to do better by your readers.

That's part of being a professional. Remember when you had work done on your home and there was a mistake? You asked them to fix it, and they did (in most cases). If you aren't satisfying your readers but they are willing to give you a second chance, don't disappoint them or you'll lose them as customers. Then you'll have to find all new customers. Isn't that fun?

All you can do with where you started and where you are is use it to help guide you in where you want to go. You can drag a book from the past and rework it to republish. Much like finding that extra burger and bag nasties in the back seat while you're on a long road trip. You eat it. Sometimes it's satisfying and other times it makes you swear off burgers. The decision is yours. The risk is yours. But the road is in front of you.

Strive for better and deliver. It's what makes us professionals.

Take control of what is in your control and do better.

POSTSCRIPT

If you liked this book, please give it a little love and leave a review. My wheelhouse is science fiction, but I have enough experience that the non-fiction makes sense and hopefully helps you. If you like this, join the 20Booksto50k® Facebook group since that's where all these conversations and explanations take place. Michael Anderle and I even have a few videos on a wide variety of self-publishing topics. You don't need to join my newsletter since I'm not going to promote non-fiction there. But if you like science fiction…

You can join my mailing list by dropping by my website www.craigmartelle.com, or if you have any comments, shoot me a note at craig@craigmartelle.com. I am always happy to hear from people who've read my work. I try to answer every email I receive.

You can also follow me on the various social media pages that I frequent.

Amazon — www.amazon.com/author/craigmartelle

Facebook —
www.faceBook.com/authorcraigmartelle
My web page — www.craigmartelle.com
Twitter — www.twitter.com/rick_banik

AUTHOR NOTES

I am a blue-collar author. I have a law degree, but that doesn't matter, not when it comes to writing. I'm retired from the Marine Corps, which means that no matter how bad things get, I've seen worse, and no matter how much I want to, I will never forget. That's one of the reasons I'm compelled to give back to the community I embrace as my own. The community of self-published authors, but that also means I've been given the opportunity to put the lessons I've learned over my lifetime into practice.

Failure is a part of learning. I've had my ups and downs in the leadership positions I've filled over the decades. I still do, but I have a lot more ups than downs nowadays. I find the most joy in seeing others succeed. One team, rising together.

That's how I define success.

Leadership is about the vision and inspiration, and that's what makes it different from management.

Shout out to the review crew! Thank you all. You helped make this book better through your valuable input. Anyone who picks up *Leader Within* will be less confused because of you. I hope we've answered most, if not all, of your questions while setting you on a better path for those who are counting on you.

Peace, fellow humans

Craig Martelle

CRAIG MARTELLE'S OTHER BOOKS
(LISTED BY SERIES)
#—AVAILABLE IN AUDIO, TOO

Terry Henry Walton Chronicles (#) (co-written with Michael Anderle)—a post-apocalyptic paranormal adventure

Gateway to the Universe (#) (co-written with Justin Sloan & Michael Anderle)—this book transitions the characters from the Terry Henry Walton Chronicles to The Bad Company

The Bad Company (#) (co-written with Michael Anderle) —a military science fiction space opera

Judge, Jury, & Executioner (#)—a space opera adventure legal thriller

Shadow Vanguard—a Tom Dublin space adventure series

Superdreadnought (#)—an AI military space opera

Metal Legion (#)—a military space opera

Battleship: Leviathan—a military science fiction series published by Aethon Books

The Free Trader (#)—a young adult science fiction action-adventure

Cygnus Space Opera (#)—a young adult space opera (set in the Free Trader universe)

Darklanding (#) (co-written with Scott Moon)—a space western

Mystically Engineered (co-written with Valerie Emerson) —mystics, dragons, & spaceships

Metamorphosis Alpha—stories from the world's first science fiction RPG

The Expanding Universe—science fiction anthologies

Krimson Empire (co-written with Julia Huni)—a galactic race for justice

Zenophobia (#)—a space archaeological adventure

End Times Alaska (#)—a Permuted Press publication—a post-apocalyptic survivalist adventure

Nightwalker (a Frank Roderus series)—A post-apocalyptic western adventure

End Days (#) (co-written with E.E. Isherwood)—a post-apocalyptic adventure

Successful Indie Author (#)—a non-fiction series to help self-published authors

Monster Case Files (co-written with Kathryn Hearst)—A Warner twins mystery adventure

Rick Banik (#)—Spy & terrorism action adventure

Ian Bragg Thrillers—a man with a conscience who kills bad guys for money

Published exclusively by Craig Martelle, Inc

The Dragon's Call by Angelique Anderson & Craig A. Price, Jr.—an epic fantasy quest

A Couples Travel—a non-fiction travel series

For a complete list of Craig's books, stop by his website —https://craigmartelle.com

Printed in Great Britain
by Amazon